The American College President

The American College President

by HAROLD W. STOKE, *President*
QUEENS COLLEGE NEW YORK CITY

HARPER & BROTHERS PUBLISHERS NEW YORK

To
PERSIS
and
MARCIA

THE AMERICAN COLLEGE PRESIDENT

Copyright © 1959 by Harold W. Stoke
Printed in the United States of America
All rights in this book are reserved. No part of the book may be used or reproduced in any manner whatsoever without written permission except in the case of brief quotations embodied in critical articles and reviews. For information address Harper & Brothers, 49 East 33rd Street, New York 16, N. Y.

FIRST EDITION

A-I

The Library of Congress catalog entry for this book appears at the end of the text.

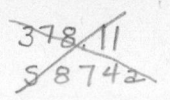

Contents

	Preface	vii
I.	The Vested Authority	1
II.	Personal Problems	21
III.	The Administrator	34
IV.	"Everything Takes Money"	54
V.	Boards of Trustees	71
VI.	Public Relations	89
VII.	Among the Scholars	106
VIII.	The Students	129
IX.	The Uneasy Campus	146
X.	The Uses of a Philosophy of Education	161
	Index	177

Preface

HIGHER education in the United States is now compulsory. It became compulsory when we began to realize that the nation could not survive without it. As a consequence colleges and universities have been transformed from institutions which are merely useful into institutions which are indispensable.

Upon the college presidents of the country, more than upon any other group of persons, falls the responsibility for the well-being of higher education. Theirs is not, fortunately for them, a sole responsibility, but the presidents do stand at the point where the myriad forces which shape higher education converge. A book about college presidents is a book about higher education. Seen from a distance the picture of the college president seems firm and clear; on closer inspection it becomes an intricate pattern of tracings in which personality, tradition, legal responsibility, and public interest blend.

The life of a college president is exciting, but the excitement is hard to capture within the covers of a book. The emotional intensities evaporate, and experiences which may turn a president's hair white will, in the telling, scarcely turn another's head. There is much that cannot be told; the vivid illustrations with names, dates, and institutions must be regretfully omitted. Furthermore, the college presidency is so unique, so different from all other academic positions, that a full appreciation of its distinction requires personal initiation. It is among those things for which experience alone is the best teacher. The position of the college president cannot be understood through the techniques of research, statistical analysis, and case studies.

This book is not a guide to the would-be college president, nor a handbook on how to administer the office. It is meant, rather, as an interpretation of an important part of higher education, a report on some of the problems of the president, and an indication of some of the pleasures and pains of his position.

College presidents do not operate in a vacuum; hence in describing them it has been necessary to talk about the intellectual, social and traditional atmosphere in which they live. These comments are actually intended for everyone—administrator, faculty member, alumnus, trustee, and the general reader—who is genuinely concerned about the improvement of American higher education. While presidents bear heavy responsibility for what happens to our colleges and universities, others, and particularly trustees, bear a heavy responsibility for what happens to presidents. Much of what is said here about college presidents is meant for others to overhear.

A book of this kind inescapably involves personal experience and observations. These have been acquired in both public and private colleges and universities, as professor, dean, and president. Where my own experiences have been drawn upon they have been compared with those of others and verified by the confidential discussions which college presidents reserve for themselves. The helpful comments of former presidential colleagues, as the manuscript emerged, have assured me that presidential problems vary less in principle than in detail. Although these and other creditors are unnamed my debts to them are large.

The president of an educational institution probably gets more education than does anyone else (with the possible exception of his wife)—almost everyone contributes to it, intentionally or not. To the host of people who have made contributions to my own education I am deeply grateful.

HAROLD W. STOKE
New York City, 1958

I

The Vested Authority

It is invariably the president who pronounces the magic formula, "By virtue of the authority vested in me I confer upon you the degree...." From the commencement platforms of hundreds of colleges and universities each year these dignified and official-sounding words are addressed to thousands of self-conscious students, their beaming parents and admiring friends, and to an entire society which, like an invisible, ghostly presence, hovers over the occasion.

They are not idle words. The instant they are pronounced they end the careers of students who have long been engaged in courses of study of varying degrees of difficulty and with varying degrees of success, and inaugurate the careers of bachelors of arts and science, doctors of philosophy, lawyers, engineers, doctors, dentists, and teachers with, as the magic formula further tells them, "all the rights and privileges appertaining thereto."

At the moment, however, it is upon the president that all eyes are fixed and all attention is focused. He speaks for all higher education, for the faculty who have certified the competence of the students, for the trustees who have vested their authority in him, and for the society whose support, public or private, maintains the institution. On such dramatic occasions it is possible to see how much of the entire system of higher education centers around the lone figure in his colorful cap and gown, the American college president.

College presidents are conspicuous figures in American life. There are many of them; they preside over approximately eighteen hundred colleges and universities, and in each the position of the president is unique. The institution may have ten faculty members or a thousand, a hundred students or twenty thousand, but it has only one president. And the presidents are as important as they are conspicuous, because the institutions over which they preside are important, and because their responsibilities for those institutions are heavier than those of anyone else.

The public's picture of college presidents, like its pictures of most public figures, is not clear. The college president of a generation or two ago was, in the popular mind, the embodiment of dignity, respectability, and wisdom. Since higher education was dominated by or closely associated with religion, the college president was usually a minister, chosen as the most learned or the most zealous among his colleagues. His qualifications for handling chapel services or teaching moral philosophy, or for setting an example of personal dignity and deportment for the young, were far more important than administrative experience. It is interesting to note that Woodrow Wilson was the first nonclerical president at Princeton; and Harvard always had ministerial presidents until Charles Eliot. Yale did not break the tradition until 1899, and Dartmouth until 1916.

While something of this heritage still lingers about the college president, it is now only a kind of after-image of an academic life which has all but disappeared. Higher education today has become more secular than religious; it has expanded incredibly in volume and variety; its purposes and intellectual preoccupations are different and more numerous than they used to be, and the sheer bulk of its property, population, expenditures, and responsibilities has become an inextricable part of national living.

This transformation of colleges and universities reflects itself in the position of their presidents, and has brought to that position men whose training, interests, and skills are far different from those of their predecessors. The college president as the Man of Learning has been giving way to the Man of Management, although the change has not taken place without strain and conflict.

Two opposing views of college presidents prevail. Some see them as fervent, dedicated men who carry their great responsibilities because they believe, in President Robert Hutchins' words, that "Education may not save us, but it is the only hope we have." Others see these same presidents as furious promoters, hucksters of the educational world, timid or pompous as the occasion requires, and with no real appreciation for the work of scholars and teachers. To paraphrase the remarks of Thomas Paine about George Washington (and perhaps with no greater justification), they profess to be puzzled as to whether the college president has abandoned good principles, or never had any.

In any case, no one will understand the college president in America, his services and his responsibilities, without understanding the nature of colleges and universities themselves. The men and their institutions are inseparable and, in the pages which follow, the discussion is frequently about American education as well as about the position of the college president. The one cannot be understood apart from the other. We must begin with a few facts and observations about the institutions.

The first fact of transcendent importance is that the eighteen hundred colleges and universities in America are attended by more than three million students in various stages of explosive adolescence and developing maturity. The colleges have a kind of national guardianship of the country's future brain power. The students and the institutions they attend mirror every interest of

American society. Diversity of background and purpose is as true of the schools as it is of the students. The colleges vary in size; of the eighteen hundred institutions, two hundred and thirty of them do about seventy per cent of the work of higher education for the country. About two-thirds of these colleges and universities are private (most of these are "church-related"), and about one-third are public. The public institutions, however, now enroll more than fifty per cent of the students, and their proportion is slowly rising. It seems a certainty that by 1965 there will be five million students in college-grade institutions, as eloquent a commentary on our country and on the age as one could devise. In the education of these students the colleges and universities will have to wrap up the skills and wisdom sufficient not only to sustain the present but to bring about the future. It is a thrilling responsibility—for those who thrive on responsibility.

Higher education has become big business and the period of expansion just ahead will make the present pale by comparison. The annual investment in college plants and facilities begins to read like a public works program (indeed, it is!); the capital budget for the University of California alone over the next five years is projected at 175 million dollars, and Harvard has recently embarked on a campaign for 82 million dollars, half of which must go into new buildings. The annual payments by students and parents for tuition, board and room, the salaries of faculty and staff, the millions in scholarships and research subsidies, to say nothing of federal aid and private philanthropy, will make higher education in the future an instrument even more efficient for redistributing the national wealth than it is now. The first revolution in American education came with Horace Mann's insistence that to be democratic our society must be literate, and consequently, that education for literacy must be universal and compulsory. The second revolution came with the dawning realization in the 1940s that education is not an expense to be kept as low as possible, but an investment which holds out a promise of compound interest. Education, including higher education, really became compulsory when we began to discover how much the maintenance of our national life depends on it. Our society was not produced nor can it be continued by ignoramuses.

In the educational explosion following World War II, the G.I. Bill of Rights played a tremendous role. In addition to providing hundreds of thousands of young people with an education they would otherwise have missed, it insured that their youngsters, too, would go to college, returning in 1965, like salmon to their home streams, to the very campuses on which, in the postwar period, they were born. Strange parents and rare, in this age, who want less education for their children than they had for themselves!

Yet the colleges and universities are important for more than merely the size of the streams of money and people which flow through them. Academic people themselves are now sufficiently numerous and active in the entire society to be a major factor in setting the tone and tastes of their communities. "Brain-truster" and "egg-head" are not wholly terms of derision; they carry overtones, perhaps grudging, of recognition and even respect. (We frequently hear the complaint that the teacher is not respected in America, but haven't all professions felt the leveling effects of equalitarianism?) Town and gown are more indistinguishable than they once were and this is itself a testimony to the rising level of education. If college professors are more like townspeople, townspeople are also more like college professors.

I have noticed that every town which can call itself a "college town" takes pride in doing so. Every doctor, teacher, lawyer, minister, engineer or other professional now owes his status and his training to some college or university. As the professional and white-collar groups grow proportionately larger in our population, the influence of the colleges and universities expands.

Finally, no small part of what the nation reads, says, and thinks is supplied and shaped by the books, lectures, and investigations of its academic scholars. No wonder there is a steady increase of public interest and concern in what scholars write and say, and in the academic freedom they must have. If colleges and universities were not important the public would not worry about them.

All of this, of course, has been true in some degree since colleges and universities began. The difference is that in these days the part they play is much larger and much more self-conscious than it used to be. We now know more about the importance of education, that it is not something merely pleasant to have, but something indispensable for survival. Hence the institutions which provide the indispensable education themselves become indispensable, and so do the people who run them. If the public is growing more concerned about higher education it is because of the growing realization that we cannot live without it. We had better learn to live with—and to cherish—what we cannot live without.

Within the last generation, higher education has not only expanded in size, it has been transformed as to what it does. It is doing far more things than it ever did before. No matter what kind of vacuum develops in American life, the colleges and universities, being full of mission-minded people, rush to fill it. The result, especially among the larger institutions, is that higher education reflects almost every activity in American life, with the possible exception of fraud and violence. The whole population seems to be coming back to school in some form of adult education. The R.O.T.C. programs of the Army, Navy, and Air Force, in times of peace, train more officers in the five hundred and forty-three colleges and universities in which they have units than do the regular military services themselves, including West Point, Annapolis, and the new Air Force Academy. Farmers and businessmen are always at home in the land-grant colleges and in university schools of business. Services of every variety—reading and speech clinics, cancer examinations, psychological clinics, tractor and materials testing, lectures and concerts—involve a range of interests from medicine to liberal arts and are frequently designed as much or more for a general public than for a college-age clientele. Through the annual expenditure of 350 million dollars in contract research in institutions of higher education, the federal government has established virtual branches of the armed services on many campuses and, directly or indirectly, supports the development of the sciences in every college in the land. The physics departments of any of the major universities of the country—California, Illinois, M.I.T., Columbia, Michigan—would be shadows of their present selves if the support of national agencies were withdrawn. Summer schools, institutes, and training and refresher programs are forms of public service as much or more than they are forms of conventional academic study. For years, of course, intercollegiate athletics, especially football, has been taken over by the public for its own entertainment, although it good-naturedly allows the schools to retain the belief (and even pretends to share it) that the games are still student recreation! So diverse have the activities of higher education become that it is not unfair to say that our colleges and universities, especially our large ones, are being transformed into general public service institutions which still include the education of the young as one —but only one—of their important responsibilities.

It would be easy to accept, and thus dismiss, these developments in our colleges and universities as a normal expression of American pragmatic social philosophy. While European universities with their class-conscious traditions have been historically far removed from the lives of the masses, American universities in their yearning to be of service to a democratic society tend to be all things to all men. How nearly can they do so and yet remain distinctively educational institutions?

As a practical matter the answer to the question has important consequences. The ever-widening services of the colleges and universities diffuse the resources of higher education, undermine its sense of priorities, keep faculties more poorly paid than they might otherwise be, and reduce the effectiveness of all its activities by overburdening staffs and facilities.

The intellectual consequences may be even more serious. In the minds of students, faculty, and the general public, the belief grows steadily that whatever is carried on in an educational institution is, by definition, educational. Moreover, whatever is educational is entitled to equal status and respect. An educational philosophy which can include embalming, cosmetology, flower arranging, and supermarketry among the responsibilities of higher education tends to see every activity as equally important. By identifying them with higher education, the result is not to raise the esteem in which these familiar services are held but to reduce the esteem in which more purely intellectual activities are held. The long and painful processes by which concepts and generalizations are built in mathematics, science, philosophy, law, and history are in sharp contrast with the obvious "efficiency" of applied knowledge. The public supports the practical and the useful more readily than it supports the theoretical, the value of which is more difficult to appreciate.

Our potpourri of higher education has other questionable consequences. One of these is an unfortunate spirit of commercialism —a tendency to prepare and to offer to students and to the public the educational packages of greatest institutional self-interest. Public institutions are tempted to include, or to accept, in their range of interests studies, activities, or services which will win for them support from some segment of the public which would not otherwise be at all concerned about higher education. This is illustrated in a number of states where colleges of agriculture receive support from organized horse racing, or where a tax on liquor may be dedicated to medical research.

THE VESTED AUTHORITY

For private institutions the temptation is to provide a home for any reasonably respectable program, from book publishing to jewelry manufacturing, for which donors are willing to pay. Even if the immediate program is of no great intrinsic educational interest, the theory is that the acceptance of these gifts is likely to attract more desirable ones—incidentally, a highly dubious theory.

No respectable college or university in America will deliberately sell a degree, but the services they sometimes provide aim at genuine financial profit to the institution. Credits obtainable by the most diverse methods and by variable fees, intensive recruitment of students, persuasive advertising, and the constant creation of appealing courses and curricula make some of the activities of higher education hard to distinguish from other kinds of business. The invitation to learning is often made so attractive and its difficulty made so obscure that many people accept it under serious illusions. American higher education has not yet found the royal road to learning, but its failure to do so is not for lack of trying.

Such are the new and changing institutions which college presidents now head. It would be strange if the management of such institutions did not require a multitude of new skills as well as new and different qualities of mind and character in those who direct them.

Yet before we can concentrate our attention on the presidents there is one other significant fact about higher education that we must ponder. This is the change in the product it now turns out —the new definition of the educated man. The end product of the colleges and universities is no longer Learning, but Competence, competence defined, to be sure, not in narrow but in broad terms. This change is the result of a combination of subtle and compelling factors—the expansion and specialization of knowledge, the pressure by and upon students for the marketability of education, the subdivision of schools and disciplines, the passionate pursuit of personal distinction and reputation among faculty members, and a declining appreciation for some of the older forms of learning. The change in our definition of the educated man from the man of learning to the man of competence has had some profound effects upon higher education itself. The curriculum has mushroomed into an amazing volume and variety of forms. New schools have leaped into being. Old subjects, such as English and history, are being refashioned into the arts of communication and social interpretation.[1] The sciences proliferate and flourish. No student can take a fraction of the courses open to him. The educated man today is a specialist. If he is well educated he has probably, in addition, developed a hobby; if he is *very* well educated he has also made a specialty of his hobby! The educated man must know a great deal about his own field, but he must also know enough to apologize (and usually does!) when he gets outside it.

It is important to know this much, at least, about colleges and universities if we are going to understand their presidents and some of the problems confronting them. It is around the president that this St. Vitus dance of activity and crushing conflict of interest swirls. In the eyes of the public he is responsible for everything about the place, good or bad. The institution is *his*—the faculty, the grounds and buildings, the football team—and he is held responsible for it. On the campus, *his* is the responsibility for the food in the dining halls, for the level of salaries, for the elegance of commencement occasions. The spotlight of publicity plays upon him so continuously that it leaves him not even intermittent shadows within which he and his family may make an unmarked move.

Who are the men who hold these exacting positions? How are

[1] The dean of a major arts college recently told me he saw no reason for studying Shakespeare unless Shakespeare had "something to say about our modern problems."

they placed there? What qualifications do they have? How does higher education look from their vantage point? What are the prizes and pains of their positions? And what happens to them when they leave their posts?

At this point any reader might reasonably ask how one can write about college and university presidents as though they were all alike, when men and institutions appear to differ so widely. College presidents *are* all alike in that the nature of their offices is determined by the functions they perform and not by the size and diversity of their institutions. Parents are parents whether they have one child or thirteen. Swarthmore College is obviously not the University of California, yet the president of Swarthmore does for his institution exactly what the president of California does for his.

Differences in size are not differences in nature; differences in organization and administrative techniques are more nearly differences in detail than in principle. Indeed, there may be no less art and no less strain in the administration of the smaller as against the larger institution. Painting a miniature may be no less exacting than producing a mural; the military skill of a general is not proportional to the number of his divisions. It is not the size of the realms that produces the fellow-feeling among royalty. It is not the *size* of the schools, but the similarity of their missions which makes the problems of college presidents astonishingly alike.[2]

How does a college president get his job? He gets it not necessarily because he wants it but because other people want him to have it. As in the case of the President of the United States, the principle which governs the search for college presidents is that

[2] Professor John O'Hara, after twenty-seven years at the University of Chicago, spent a year as a Whitney visiting distinguished professor at the College of Idaho to get "the feel of a small college." He told me of his astonishment at discovering the remarkable similarity of the problems of the presidents of the two institutions.

the job must seek the man—and the principle operates in about the same way. Men who want to be President of the United States find ways of letting the fact be known, and men interested in becoming college presidents have ways of becoming "visible" in places where presidents are customarily looked for. Yet the sensitivities of academic life are stubborn facts and the man who offends them by pursuing too openly his ambition to be a college president is likely to end up thrice a bridesmaid.

The legal power to select the president is vested in the board of trustees; but the actual process of selection is not simple. Whether the board chooses to carry on its search openly, in consultation with faculty, alumni, or public, or whether it keeps its own counsel, it will find itself the center of attention, the object of gratuitous suggestions and advice, and the focus of direct or indirect campaigns. Negotiations under such circumstances with prospective presidents require the qualifications of diplomacy, politics, and Oriental marriage brokerage. If a desirable nominee is already a president of a college, he must be approached cautiously, lest damaging rumors that he is dissatisfied reach his own institution. Again, no nominee wants to find out that he is a second choice, that the job has already been offered to and refused by someone else; yet the institution, in turn, must protect itself against being turned down, for fear it may quickly get a reputation as a place top-flight men are avoiding. Moreover, the knowledge that a given name is under consideration sets off activity and counter-activity. If a board selects a candidate without consultation, the newly appointed president may find himself as welcome among alumni and faculty as an uninvited guest. Wide consultation, on the other hand, may merely intensify partisanship and result in a compromise selection, for whom or against whom little or nothing can be said. No wonder boards of trustees heave a heavy sigh when they start the search for a new president, and a sigh of relief when they find him.

THE VESTED AUTHORITY

Yet, somehow the choice gets made, long, involved, and tedious as the process may be, and from the selections it is possible to identify some of the preferred qualities and qualifications. What are they?

Look again at the analogy of the President of the United States. There are probably twenty million men in the United States who are legally qualified to be President, that is, they are native-born citizens who are thirty-five years of age. How does it happen that every four years only a handful of these millions of citizens emerge for serious consideration? The formal, legal qualifications are simple; it is the "plus factors" of intelligence, experience, personality, and luck which make a man President of the United States. So it is with college presidents. Inside and outside academic communities are hundreds of thousands of persons of the right age and formal education to become college presidents, but the search goes on endlessly for the happy combination of plus factors. Finding that combination is likely to be fortuitous, for there is no formal training school for college presidents.

Why isn't there a school for training future college presidents?[3] For the same reasons, I suspect, that there is no school for training

[3] The nearest approach to such a school is a summer institute for college presidents which has been operated since 1955 under the leadership of Professor Robert W. Merry at Harvard, with financial support from the Carnegie Corporation. It is not for the prospective or would-be college president but for those who are relatively new in their positions. Together with their wives, the fledgling presidents are invited to study their common problems. The "course" consists of lectures from experienced or retired college presidents, from representatives of associated or interested groups, such as boards of trustees, alumni, and laymen. Considerable emphasis is put on actual but disguised case studies of academic freedom, relations to boards of trustees, public relations, and the like.

The institute, although experimental, appears to have demonstrated its value. Those who have attended it say they seldom found answers to their own specific problems, but they gained confidence from learning how well, or badly, others handle theirs. One of the greatest values is psychological, coming from the realization, as each returns to his own post, that his problems are not quite so unique as he might otherwise have supposed.

future congressmen. The requirements of each constituency differ a little from those of every other. The processes of selection are too capricious, the chances of selection too remote. The factors which make a distinguishable college president, or congressman, are factors of individuality which are too intricate a compound of heredity, environment, personality, and experience ever to be reduced to a curriculum. There are many things a college president must learn, but they are not things which are reducible to a curriculum—and who could teach them?

Of course, there are many things which, if a college president knows in advance of his appointment, he will find useful—things about faculties, students, curricula, and colleges generally, as against mastery of a single professional field. Yet, oddly enough, there is no discernible evidence (although I must leave it to the reader to supply illustrations from his own acquaintance with college presidents) that those presidents who have come to their offices through a long apprenticeship of academic, or other, administrative experience are more successful than those who have not. The moral is, I suppose, that that which makes an artist distinctive is not learned from someone else, and that ducks do not have to be taught to swim.[4]

Yet just as surely as any group—ministers, politicians, or airplane pilots—reveal the marks of their calling, so do college presidents. Underneath the professionalism of manner imposed upon them by the pressures of their offices, they display noticeable distinctions and similarities. They are, for example, above average

[4] For some years the Carnegie Corporation has made annually three or four small travel grants to "promising" young college administrators, nominated by various persons or institutions. A considerable number of these young men have subsequently become college or university presidents. It is far more likely, I think, that it was the combination of qualities which led people to nominate them originally rather than any experience under their grants which led to their eventual selections as college presidents. The travel grants did increase their "visibility," however, and also provided the recipients with much useful information.

in their physical vigor, their "capacity to take it." They talk easily, but warily. More skillfully than most men, they can make words do their bidding—idly filling the time, concealing their thoughts, or serving a purpose. They are alert, always conscious of the people around them. They tend to be extroverts, less wearied than most by human contacts. Cheerfulness and optimism are parts of their personal and professional equipment, for their work requires that they be promotional-minded. "Personable" and "charming" are descriptive words that come to mind, for these qualities are more frequently present than absent.

When these personal decorations and qualities are found combined with the necessary formal educational requirements, a scandal-free personal reputation, some administrative experience, a degree of honesty, sincerity, and a feeling for justice, the heart is ready to leap up in recognition of the ideal college president. The search, as the elder Walpole described it, is for the administrator who, in addition to a respectable life and an acceptable education, has "good faith, good manners, good humor, and good sense."

If I were to make a general observation about the qualifications of college presidents, it would be this: in recent years the factor of educational distinction has declined while factors of personality, management skills, and successful experience in business and administration have increased in importance. This fact reflects the gradual transformation of the college president from an intellectual leader into a manager, skilled in administration, a broker in personal and public relations.

Yet, despite the growing emphasis upon qualifications of personality and administrative skill rather than upon scholarly achievements, the choice of college presidents is still made more frequently (since the decline of the ministry) from the general liberal arts than from the professional academic fields, or from business or politics. Presently there are two medical men among presidents of the major universities; usually there are none. Engineers are rarely chosen, except as heads of technical schools; business is growing in its representation, but it is still a tiny minority; and after wars there have always been a few college presidents chosen from among military figures. The recent choices in college presidents are less dependent on the fields from which they were drawn than on the personal and intellectual qualifications which were sought.

No matter what his qualifications may be, however, the actual choice of a college president will, by virtue of the methods of selection, be subject to the laws of chance. There will never be a dearth of nominees or candidates—the number who suggest themselves is substantial. Even a small college may have as many as a hundred names suggested to it, and among men equally well qualified the choice may turn upon the caprice of hearsay, the incidental impression, the tenacity of a particular board member, or some unpredictable factor. When perfection is the goal, even the slightest imperfection may be fatal. The Fates must wear their most inscrutable smiles over the selection of college presidents.

Of course, various institutions want various combinations of plus factors in their presidents and occasionally specify a special qualification. A liberal arts college may want a somewhat different background or experience from that which a state university seeks; a denominational school must keep its distinctive concerns in mind when it searches for the right man. After twenty years of scientific emphasis under President Conant, Harvard may want a revival of the humanities under President Pusey. Chicago, after a series of stable and conventional administrations, obviously wanted to take a chance on adventure under President Hutchins. Michigan, after excitement with Clarence Cook Little, sought peace under President Ruthven. Sometimes a university deliberately seeks to capitalize on an established reputation, as did Columbia in choosing General Eisenhower and the University of Pennsylvania in Governor Stassen. Or, it may promote men who, not well known outside its walls, were well and favorably known within, as did Yale with President Griswold, M.I.T. with President Killian, and Princeton with President Goheen.[5]

College presidents hold precarious jobs, and this fact affects every aspect of the office. Academic tenure is not for presidents; they hold office at "the pleasure of the Board." The average term in recent decades is about four years, and if it were not for the exceptional records of such stalwarts as Butler at Columbia (forty-four years), Hopkins at Dartmouth (twenty-nine years) and Sproul at California (twenty-eight years), the average would be much less. College presidents change almost as frequently as football coaches.

While terms of service may tend to be more stable in some colleges and universities, and particularly in the Ivy League, the real surprise is that even there terms are no longer than they are. Johns Hopkins has had five presidents in the past twenty-five years, and since President Butler left in 1950, Columbia has had four presidents or acting presidents. Illinois has also had in recent years a succession of presidents and acting presidents. And while many colleges and universities have excellent records of presidential stability, this fact only emphasizes the widespread instability which produces the national average. For some years, the presi-

[5] The tendency to select nonacademic men as presidents of colleges and universities was bitterly attacked by the late Dr. Monroe Deutsch, Provost of the University of California. He said. "After all, is not educational leadership the prime qualification we seek in a president? In the past we could point to many such great figures—Eliot of Harvard, Gilman of Johns Hopkins, Angell of Michigan, Harper of Chicago, Wheeler of California, Jordan of Stanford—and each of these was a Scholar, not a businessman, a lawyer, a general or a politician. Indeed, I wonder whether the present trend in our universities toward the choice of presidents primarily on the basis of administrative ability may not be responsible for the fact that we can today count our outstanding presidents on the fingers of one hand whereas three or four decades ago two or more hands would have been required." "Choosing College Presidents," *School and Society*, vol. 66, p. 308, October 25, 1947.

dents of the National Association of State Universities have played a kind of game with themselves, listing their members each year in the order of their seniority. It is interesting to see how quickly newcomers shoot toward the top. At the meeting of the Association in 1957, of fifty members five new members had joined in the last eight months and only nineteen of the fifty state university presidents had been in office as much as ten years. (By September of 1958, ten of the fifty had retired, resigned, or been replaced!) Retirement for age or health, death, raids by other institutions, politics, and voluntary and involuntary resignations decimate the ranks.[6]

This precariousness of tenure has an important effect upon the institution and upon the personality and policies of the president himself. It takes time to effect educational programs, and changes of presidents disturb continuity. Interregnums are periods of uncertainty; they encourage rivalries and conflicts of interests. The momentum of desirable programs slows down. Institutions and presidents ought not, but frequently do, change their relations for light and transient reasons.[7]

[6] It is a staggering thought, but it is a fact that, on the average, about 350 new college presidents have to be recruited each year in the United States! The late President Tressider of Stanford explained the four-year term humorously as follows: The first year, the president spends his honeymoon on the campus. The second year, he finds himself interested in questions which take him away from the campus. The third year, he finds himself concerned with matters of broad national interest. And the fourth year, he spends looking for a new job!

[7] Likewise, retirements or resignations announced far in advance have disrupting consequences. The incumbent can reasonably explain postponements of decisions as matters proper for his successor; and many proposals will not be made at all in the hope that the known views of one administration will be replaced by those of a more favorable one. As the term of a president nears its end his administration naturally becomes tentative and indecisive, and thought and attention are fixed on his successor. Furthermore, the lingering relinquishment of power stimulates factionalism, crystallizes criticism of the president in office, and makes subsequent institutional unity more difficult to achieve. I have known instances where for as much as two years colleges have been distracted by intrigue and dissension. On

Precariousness in office may also diminish the vigor and modify the policies of a president during his tenure. A whisper that a president does not enjoy the confidence of his board can affect his command over his entire responsibilities. Quite naturally, therefore, a president who holds his position at the "pleasure of the board" will, if he wishes to continue in his job, see to it that it is the board's pleasure that he does so. He will be tempted to pull his punches, always to play safe. And if he actually needs the job, this temptation will be overwhelming. I know one president who maintained what he called a Go-to-Hell Fund, enough to enable him to move and to spend six months looking for another job. Independence of mind is a noble quality, but it does not exist in a vacuum.

Presidential insecurity, however, is not merely a matter of money. The stake of a president in his job is high. If he values his own intellectual honesty he has placed himself in a position where it will be sorely tried. If there is trouble of any kind the consequences for him will be serious. No other college wants a president who has a record of difficulty; there is always the supposition that had he been wiser he might have prevented trouble. If he resigns his position in defense of educational convictions, he will immediately become a controversial figure, criticized by all who do not share his convictions. A college president risks the integrity of his convictions, the possibility of failure or at least of getting a reputation for failure, the unlikelihood of securing comparable employment, and, as Bacon said, he takes the chance of being the spectator at the funeral of his own reputation. In the language of business, it is a high-risk occupation in which the college president must write his own insurance. Such considera-

---

the other hand, resolute and well-timed relinquishments coupled with prompt selection of successors have also been accomplishd as, for example, in the case of Presidents Hopkins and Dickey at Dartmouth, Conant and Pusey at Harvard, and many others. Readers will be able to supply their own illustrations of both situations.

tions as these used to lead President Walter Jessup of the Carnegie Corporation more often than not to advise young men not to allow themselves to become interested in college presidencies.

Why does a man want to be a college president? Bacon said, "The legitimate end of ambition is to do good," but that was before modern psychology had shown how intricate human motives really are. All the values highly regarded by society play their part—power, prestige, money—as well as the desire to be of service. Probably the most important factor is the restlessness in men which arises from the sense of unused powers and energies. President Dykstra of Wisconsin used to say, "Any man around this university has something wrong with him if by the time he is forty he doesn't believe he can get behind my desk and do a better job than I can."

In all fairness it must be said that the men who are willing or eager to get behind the presidential desk usually have some ideas as to an educational job they believe in and want to see accomplished. And there are obscure impulses in human nature which possess channel swimmers and mountain climbers and, perhaps, the men who become college presidents, impulses to adventure and danger. Danger offers exhilaration; risks and rewards are usually equated. John Erskine once remarked that being a college president was like a small boy walking a high picket fence—thrilled, but in constant danger of being impaled.

Exciting, exacting, exhausting—it is probably these very characteristics of the college presidency which attract those who are eager to try it. But the position is full of paradoxes—those who enjoy it are not very successful, and those who are successful are not very happy. The explanation is hidden somewhere in the philosophy of power. Those who enjoy exercising power shouldn't have it, and those who should exercise it are not likely to enjoy it. One thing is clear: colleges must have presidents and it makes a great difference who they are!

II

The President's Personal Problems

"Young man, you have changed your profession"; such was greeting of an old college president to a new one. No new president is ever quite prepared for the complete shock of this truth. He has thought excitedly about his administrative duties and his new educational interests, but he cannot anticipate the extent to which he will have to be a new person and lead a new life. He is now clothed in garments of dignity and authority. For a time he is likely to be self-conscious about them, and he finds that other people are even more so. So long as he wears them, however, he will find that they have their effects; wise is the man who knows how to wear them to produce only the effects they should have, and no others.

A new president's first discoveries are little ones. He finds himself the object of new and flattering attentions. His little jokes and witticisms are greeted with more laughter than they are worth—"loyalty laughter," some genius has called it. His opinions carry more weight; he may freely interrupt other conversations, but his own must not be interrupted. His casual questions may be interpreted as the forerunners of an investigation, and a complimentary or critical remark will sprout wings and fly immediately to its object. At any social gathering he is scrutinized for signs of health, weariness, pleasure, or boredom, and others always walk the second mile for his convenience.

These intimate little discoveries are but the advance notices of more serious ones. The first and most shocking is the loss of his freedom of speech. It is a wonderful paradox that the more power, the less freedom; that the man who theoretically should be able to say whatever comes into his mind actually has the least freedom of speech of all. The college president begins to understand Rousseau: one thinks himself the master of others, yet remains a greater slave than they.

Aside from official, channeled communications, the job of carrying on conversation between a president and members of his faculty and staff is difficult. Many matters of common interest cannot be discussed. The faculty, out of deference to official reticence, must not pry, and the president, for fear of unforeseen consequences, must not comment. The burning questions of interest to both must be avoided—whether Professor X should have published his article in the *New Masses*, whether the faculty is opposed to television courses, whether there will be more money for salaries next year, whether admission requirements should be raised when the dormitories are not yet full, whether the president is making progress in getting a new dean, or whether the governor will be friendly in his next budget recommendations. I have seen a president pass through a faculty club on his way to a table and extinguish half a dozen flaming conversations, conversations which flickered back to life after he had passed but with only half their former vigor. Most presidents give up the struggle after a while and seldom appear in places where general conversation with associates takes place; they are unwilling to impose upon themselves or others the necessity for inventing the small talk which conceals the deeper concerns of both.

A college president quickly learns to be a man of calculated speech, not only in his casual conversation but in his official communications as well. A show of feeling on his part, a touch of personal sensitivity, a sarcastic quip, can alter the tone of a faculty or committee meeting and leave a residue of warning which will adversely affect future meetings. This is as true for what he writes as for what he says. The president who learns early that no letters he writes are safely private will save himself much trouble. Sooner or later the consequences of what he writes in letters or in speeches will have to be faced—he can never write without unseen readers of unknown identity looking over his shoulder, and unseen audiences will overhear what he says. Presidents must learn to say and to write nothing until they are deliberately ready to accept the consequences.

Even more dismaying is the president's discovery that he is a man of many acquaintances but few friends. The reason is simple: friendship is possible only between equals, and a college or university has only one president. Henry Adams stated long ago that a friend in power is a friend lost. If a president is chosen from within his institution, his old and close friendships will wither, and if he comes from outside, his new position will not allow him to form them. Oddly enough, the friendship of a president can even blight those to whom he might wish to extend it. Friendship with some will be construed by others as presidential favoritism, and the recipient will be the object of jealousy or be accused of self-seeking. The loss of natural friendship with close associates is a grim price but it must be paid. The first responsibility of good administration is justice, and the requirements of justice and of friendship are incompatible.

Robbed of his freedom of speech and left with acquaintances in lieu of friends, a college president, however gregarious outwardly, is a lonely man. Since, as Aristotle said, men, to live alone, must be gods or beasts, presidents escape their dilemma largely by forming their warming friendships outside academic relationships or by seeking the company of their fellow presidents. College presidents form a tight club, not because they wish to be deliberately exclusive, but because they cannot or are not allowed to be comfortable members of any club other than their own.

This is interestingly illustrated in the history of the Association of American Universities, an organization of thirty-seven of the major universities of the country. Originally an organization of graduate schools, it was at the outset attended by presidents and graduate deans upon equal terms. With the enormous increase in the complexity of universities during and after World War II, the presidents found themselves able to give less time to questions of graduate study, the original preoccupation of the Association, and found themselves burdened with problems they could not or would not discuss within the hearing of the graduate deans. Under the leadership of Presidents Conant and Hutchins, the presidents reorganized the Association, retaining the historic form but dividing the presidents and the deans into completely separate groups. Furthermore, the presidents adopted a regulation that no representative of a university except the president could attend the presidents' meeting, thus insuring the essential unity of their meetings. They likewise dispensed with formal minutes and even with a formal agenda. In taking these steps, the instincts of the presidents were sound: they cannot meet on equal terms with nonpresidents. Among themselves, college presidents can relax their wariness and reserve, relying upon the uniqueness which allows them to feel at home with each other but not with subordinates, however friendly.

Another surprising discovery for the college president is to find how little of his time, thought, and energy goes into education. Trevelyan once remarked that whenever a writer or an artist produced a work of genius, the whole world became a conspiracy to wine and dine him in order to see to it that he never did it again. So it is with college presidents. Selected as they are because it is believed that they have minds and personalities which can exert influence upon education, they find themselves absorbed in a round of social activities. Faced constantly with questions of raising money, meetings of a hundred different kinds, speeches and ceremonial occasions, and the most diverse and pressing correspondence, they seldom have a moment for reflection, much less for the planning that effective educational leadership requires.

The things people want to see a president about are almost never matters of education; they see him to evoke his power, not his thought. His correspondence and his telephone bring him the same concerns—complaints, requests, permissions, encouragements, but little opportunity to exert any effect on education, except by indirection. Assistants can relieve him but they cannot release him.

If college presidents are so overburdened, why don't they reorganize their work and distribute some of their responsibilities? It is a fair question. Many of them have thought hard about the problem and have even tried, but with negligible success. The reasons are many. There is, for example, the lag both on and off the campus in appreciating the transformation in institutions of higher education. In the minds of students, faculty, and the public, there still lingers the image of the benevolent college president taking an active personal interest in the life of everyone associated with the institution. Moreover, this particular image is hard to eradicate, even under conditions of mass education, because of the kind of *total* relationship which colleges and universities bear, especially to students and faculty. To students (and to their parents) the school inevitably stands *in loco parentis*, and it is likewise the focus around which the faculty arrange their lives. The natural implication is that there must be *someone*, that is, a *person*, at the center of so personal an enterprise. Obviously it can be no *one* but the president.

Furthermore, it is difficult to persuade people to accept the decisions of delegated authority. If there is higher authority, people want access to it, and in the academic world they want access to it freely, as a matter of courtesy and of right. President Hutchins had himself named chancellor of the University of Chicago and had another person designated as president, thinking that many of the responsibilities of the presidency would remain with the office of that title. The device fooled no one; Mr. Hutchins as president or as chancellor was still the boss and everyone knew it.[1]

At the University of California, chancellorships were created under the president of the university for the campuses at Berkeley and at Los Angeles. In this case the difficulty was that the president was reluctant to delegate authority for fear it would be permanently lost and would thus disrupt the basic unity of the university.

Sometimes a president achieves a Damon-and-Pythias relationship to some trusted provost, dean of faculty, or assistant; where he has been fortunate enough to do so, such arrangements have, perhaps, been as satisfactory a solution to his personal problem as any other. Such relationships, however, are rare and fortuitous. The real solution of the problem must wait upon more fundamental institutional evolution—genuine divisions of labor, with corresponding allocations of responsibilities and authority to offices other than the president, and the development of more adult attitudes on the part of everyone involved. The traditions of academic life will not yet, at any rate, let the president escape.

All of this is particularly galling to a man who has always thought of himself as primarily concerned with education and

[1] It is interesting to note that the position of president at the University of Chicago has not been filled since 1952.

who thought that by becoming a president he would be even more influential. He can still make noises like an educator—after all, the president can create captive audiences—but for reasons which will be seen to be fundamentally sound, he had better resign himself to a prepared fate. His personal preoccupations will no longer be those of thought and scholarship. The president has profound influence to exert upon the shape of higher education, but this does not now take traditional form.

College presidents are paid more than other people in their institutions. This is as it should be, for their jobs are infinitely more demanding than any others in academic life. Furthermore, the presidential salary buys the services of two people: the position is almost as demanding for his wife as it is for him. A salary high enough to relieve the president of serious anxieties about making ends meet is good institutional sense, for he will think better about the problems of his college if relieved somewhat of worry about his own. Actually, presidential salaries cover a wide spectrum—from nothing at all (as salaries, that is) for some Catholic schools, into the ten-thousand-dollar bracket for smaller colleges, and to forty and fifty thousand dollars for major private universities such as Chicago, Harvard, New York University, and Columbia. Among state universities, salaries range from ten or twelve thousand to twenty-five thousand and even higher in California and the Big Ten. In public institutions there is more sensitivity about large salaries for the presidents, for the taxpayer keeps a sharp eye on public salaries which exceed his own. In some states, no university president can be paid more than the governor—"unseemly and impolitic"—even though the governor's salary may have been set by some constitutional provision half a century ago, or by a legislature which is self-conscious about personal expenditures.

Frequently one hears that college presidents are paid not nearly so well as their counterparts in business who hold positions of comparable magnitude and responsibility. This is true, nor should it be otherwise, for it is not the purpose of educational institutions to make money or the expectation of educators to become rich. Moreover, important factors in the take-home pay of college presidents are the fringe benefits. Often, the president is given an official residence, certain expense allowances for official entertainment, a car, perhaps even domestic help. Since these perquisites are tax-exempt, they make the rest of his salary worth considerably more to him and less to the Internal Revenue Bureau.

Oddly enough, however, these provisions for the comfort of college presidents, although they are financially advantageous, do not add as much to the president's pleasure and freedom from care as might be supposed. Education is essentially an ascetic occupation; the kinds of comforts, food, drink, houses, servants, and cars that may be provided for some presidents do not mean as much to them as they would to the country-club set. Most college presidents do not really enjoy their glass houses. They are reminded too often that their bounty is not their own.

The wife of a former president of the University of Wisconsin met this problem with rare good temper and understanding by showing her assistant hostesses, before each official reception, exactly which rugs, chairs, pictures, and beds were "ours" and which belonged to the university in order that, as hostesses, they might answer the questions of the guests.[2]

A president soon becomes aware that those perquisites tend further to separate him from the very persons with whom he wants a close understanding. His comforts make him uncomfortably self-conscious. As a president he is constantly pleading for more money for his institution, yet the car he drives and the house he lives in are better than most. That these are "essential to

[2] One instance comes to mind in which a stranger in town could not find a hotel room. He called the president of the state university and demanded "as a taxpayer" a bed for the night in the president's house.

his office" sounds hollow in his own ears (most college presidents have a streak of Puritanism in them) and he suspects it may sound even hollower in the ears of others. He knows that no assistant professor can possibly believe that the president with *his* salary can really understand the financial problems of an assistant professor or exert himself to solve them.

Here there is no formula for presidential conduct. He must learn to blend humility, generosity, sensitivity, and poise into workable relationships with his colleagues. He must remember that where much is given much is expected. He will have to find ways of giving himself so completely that even those who envy him agree that he is worth what he gets.

The personal factors about the president's position which affect him affect his family, too. On the usual campus, his children suffer the loss of their normal, cherished anonymity, with the resulting penalties either of too much attention or of too much neglect (amounting sometimes to ostracism) on the part of other children. This can be painful. When the time comes, presidents usually find it advisable to send their children to other colleges.

In some respects, the president's wife shares most of the complexities of her husband's position and has a few exclusively her own. The social and ceremonial responsibilities of the office are such that rarely does a college or university employ a president whose wife is not equipped to share the work. What a tightrope she walks! She must smile, or she is cold; yet friendliness must not be at the expense of dignity. She must learn names, faces, and facts, especially about faculty; but they must elicit from her only warmth of interest, never comment or gossip. Above all, no word of hers must betray the slightest knowledge of official affairs; yet how tenderly she must handle the weight of her influence—the programs of the faculty club, the scholarship benefits, her comments on the new murals, or the last efforts in student dramatics. Even what to wear is for the president's wife a greater puzzle than it is for other women. If she dresses inexpensively, she may be thought patronizing; if she reflects her own tastes, she will offend those who do not share them. The discipline of office is no figure of speech for presidents' wives: it is a rigorous law. Blessed is the wife who can accept her role philosophically.

The personalities of presidents are eventually shaped by the demands of their occupations. There is no escape; there are only variations in degree. The habits of reticence and of calculated personal relationships tend to destroy spontaneity and to make sincerity difficult. The presidential necessity for self-protection against curiosity and self-seeking can breed dreadful professionalism of manner: the resort to the trivial conversation piece, the dominating control of every group to avoid unsafe topics. The exercise of authority leaves its mark, and the sense of being different can create an unhealthy appetite for attention or, conversely, make one suspicious of accepting even the friendly gesture. A president who can make his way through the pitfalls of his occupation, remaining natural and unspoiled, is fortunate in his inner resources.

While these personal adjustments of a college president and his family are sometimes irksome, they are happily accompanied by other aspects of the position which help to offset them. Although the personal social life of the president is constricted, his institutional social life expands. He is in great demand for all kinds of occasions. Most presidents are, by nature, perhaps more sociably inclined than not, and even impersonal institutional social life can bring them considerable enjoyment.

Colleges, whether large or small, still retain the characteristics of a social as well as an intellectual community. Probably the self-contained social life of colleges has declined, in part because the distinctions between town and gown have become blurred. Almost everywhere, however, the president has a responsibility for official entertaining, and to carry this out he may elect a variety

THE PRESIDENT'S PERSONAL PROBLEMS

of methods and occasions. He may have large faculty receptions or small faculty dinners; he may use his own home or the college facilities. He generally tries to establish social contact with the students, accepting their invitations or extending invitations to them. There are also fixed ceremonial occasions, commencements, Mountain Day picnics, and the traditional social functions which almost every college has. Then there are nearly always regular and systematic social relations with alumni, with parents, and with other organizations.

Most of these occasions and contacts for the president come under the heading of work. It is not relaxation; he has a duty to perform. But it would be unfair to all concerned to describe the duties as unqualifiedly onerous. Almost all of these occasions quickly become a twice-told tale for the president but they are far from it for his guests. He derives his pleasure from theirs. The pride of a freshman introducing his parents, the gratitude of parents for some scholastic mercy extended to a problem child, the pleasure of younger faculty at being included in the social life of their seniors, these are warming experiences even if they are transitory. The president of every land-grant college has felt the glow of friendliness from the "farm and home" visitors who murmur their appreciation for "what you are doing for us." Institutional though the relation is, it reassures and can be deeply satisfying.

One of the most interesting things about a college is the company it keeps, the constant flow of visitors who come to its campus. There are the lecturers and concert artists, the visiting professors, the public officials, the foreign visitors, the prospective faculty members invited for inspection, representatives of professional societies and foundations, returning alumni, and the vast number of unclassified. It is the president's privilege to meet them all, and a very large proportion make the privilege a reward. If the president cannot read books, he can talk to his visitors and he can listen. A luncheon can give him a lesson on art, on politics, on the climate of the Gold Coast, or on insect life. If he encounters bores, he can comfort himself that his is the most educational position in the college and that he is getting the education. His personal curriculum is broader and his teachers are more numerous than those of anyone else in the college.

Being a public figure may not be equally enjoyable to every president, but it does bring him into contact with other public figures. It is a rich personal experience. Over the years a college president may thus meet the great personalities of his generation at home or from abroad, a privilege which he will owe largely to his position.

Nor should it be forgotten that the college president in meeting other public figures is also being met. He is a public figure, too; his visibility is high; he comes to be identified with his college, and where it is known, so is he. Thus, the range of his own acquaintance grows, and with it grow new dimensions for his own personality, his experience, his understanding, and his fame. It is a reward not specified in his contract.

Indeed, the college presidency in America must now be regarded as a national reservoir of visible and available public servants. If a governor wishes to endow a commission with status and impartiality, he is likely to seek for its head a college president. National agencies constantly turn to college presidents for target-shooting tasks—as members of advisory boards, arbitration commissions, and investigations into operations, and as representatives abroad. A few college presidents have gone into active politics; Senator Fulbright, for example. Philanthropic foundations find the experience and wisdom of college presidents indispensable. If the enlargement of life is one of the principal satisfactions, the college president is one of the more fortunate of men.

Perhaps, after all, the personal life of the college president is not much more difficult or taxing than that of men of distinction

THE PRESIDENT'S PERSONAL PROBLEMS

in any field. At least they all share in common one important problem—that of the aftermath. After the college president leaves his position, whether he retires, resigns, or is fired, life can be something of an anti-climax. No position less exacting can fully engage him. He is ill at ease as a teacher again, yet he is so conditioned to campus life that he feels himself a stranger elsewhere. He is a general who, after the excitements of campaigns, finds peace dull, an explorer who has visited lands his associates have only read about.

So long as he continues in office the thought of these possible consequences will seldom occur to him; he is too busy. As in most personal equations he will, of course, have occasions to doubt whether the costs and returns balance to his satisfaction. But, as Lord Brougham once said, if a man's life is not full of big things, it will be full of little things. The college president may be sure his life will have its share of both.

III

The President as an Administrator

Whatever visions a president may have for his college as an intellectual center, he quickly finds that the real job is to transform his visions from the abstract to the concrete. The art of doing so is called administration. The trick is to take limited sums of money, specific pieces of property, particular persons, and certain ideas and combine them in such a way that the educational results he wants actually appear. Part of the trick is not to become bewildered or overwhelmed by the numbers and different orders of the things which must be combined. One must remember what one is putting these things together for. Or, in the metaphor of Lotus D. Coffman, a former president of the University of Minnesota, a college president is like a hunter who spends ninety-five per cent of his time swatting mosquitoes, while remembering that he is where he is in order to get a shot at a moose.

The art of administration consists of arranging means to achieve some end one has in view—whether it is the manufacturing of shoes, winning a war, or running a college. To be successful an administrator must know the end he wants to reach, what

THE PRESIDENT AS AN ADMINISTRATOR

means are appropriate for reaching it, and how to make use of such means. Education, being difficult to define and obtainable by a great variety of means, makes great and complex demands upon administrators.

The unique job as an administrator which the college president can perform is to clarify the purposes which he and his colleagues are trying to serve and to select the appropriate means by which to serve them. This requires clarity of mind as well as educational convictions; but it requires more. If the president is to suffuse the college with an active sense of accomplishment he must not only make his educational philosophy clear; he must also answer his mail promptly and know how to read a financial statement.

The president of a college is a businessman. A college or a university is a major business enterprise in itself but its administration has a few complexities of its own. If the income and outgo of the average business in the United States is about $50,000 per year, almost any college in the land is above average. The larger ones—Harvard with a half billion dollars in assets, or the University of Illinois with a biennial budget of more than $100,000,000—compare in size with very big businesses indeed. Nor are any of the administrative elements of major enterprises lacking—finance, legal problems, accounting, personnel, and property. There is even plenty of competition—for students (every college wants the best ones), for faculty members, for the donor's dollar, or for a larger share of the public's support. The old taunt from the profit-making enterprise that a college president never has to meet a payroll just is not realistic.

No private business is ever faced with such intangible limitations on its freedom of action as is a college. Academic tenure restricts the right to hire and fire; all manner of limitations of gifts, income, and appropriations hampers the free management of assets; "customers"—i.e., students, alumni, parents, the public—cannot always be told they are right; academic traditions and philosophies must be ascertained and respected. There is no occasion for the man of business to patronize the college president as an administrator.

In the mastery of college administration, one of the most difficult and most important tasks for the president is to assess his own position in the web of organization and power of which he is himself a part. He needs something of the capacity which the accomplished actor has of seeing himself while at the same time taking an important part in the play. He has to find out what he can and what he cannot do. The picture in the minds of the public, and even of many faculty members, of a college president as a man who can give commands which shape all the things for which he is held responsible is quite unreal. A college is always a going concern. It is full of habits and practices to which it is accustomed and a new president cannot suddenly change them; in fact, he will not even know what they are. The institution is staffed by personalities of varying strength who are in positions of varying influence. A touchy faculty member, a thorny dean, a secretive business manager, can put detours in the otherwise straight path the president would prefer to follow. In addition, there are the factors of his own character, experience, convictions, shortcomings and aspirations. The impact of these upon a going concern creates resultant forces which are entirely unpredictable. No legal description of his authority will tell him what he can do vigorously and "safely," what he can propose with confidence, what he will have to fight for in order to do at all, and what he had better not try.

Almost every problem which reaches the president involves a subtle assessment of authority, personalities, and influence which transcend organization and legal responsibility. The problem of presidential action is not so much what he can do legally as what he can do effectively.

As a study of presidential authority consider, in our present climate of opinion, the matter of visiting speakers to the campus. Many colleges and universities vest a final responsibility in the president as to what visitors may be permitted to speak to audiences on the campus. Rarely does any question arise from the continuous flow of visiting scholars, artists, and lecturers. Yet the swirl of events or the changing concerns of the public can suddenly transform almost any public personage into a figure of controversy. An invitation, which, at one time, would pass unnoticed may, at another, be a red flag. More specifically, someone, sooner or later, invites Alger Hiss to speak at Princeton on foreign policy, or Harry Bridges is asked to speak at the University of California on labor problems.

The decision then becomes complex and sensitive. Was the invitation issued by students, and if so should they be put in their places, or should their unwisdom be tolerated? Will there be serious consequences of public criticism if the lecturer comes? Will the endurance of such criticism be a smaller price than the probable damage to principles of academic freedom if permissions are withheld? Can the president avoid involvement in the controversy in order that he may conserve his strength for more important skirmishes or is this the occasion on which he should assert his strength because he will have even less strength in the future if he does not? The president is lucky if he has sufficient previous experience, or character, or is enough of a "born administrator" to estimate the situation correctly.

No president can hope to run a college by himself, although now and then there are presidents who try. The president must have administrative help and this means organization. The organization may take different forms and may vary greatly in size, but from the president's point of view it should serve two purposes: to get the necessary work done well and promptly, and to extricate the president from the harrowing details which will otherwise defeat his efforts to make plans and give perspective to the entire enterprise. The president simply must not allow himself to be "snowed." There is basic truth for him in Beardsley Ruml's happy aphorism: "If you find yourself doing any work, you're underorganized." And the president will drown in his sea of details unless he learns to swim.

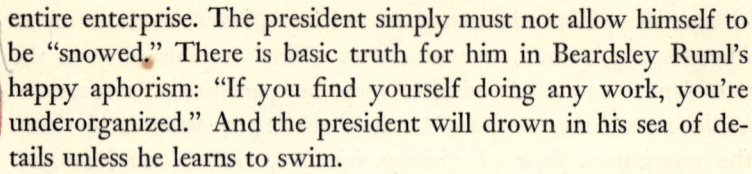

Unhappily, it must be admitted that some college presidents, in common with some other executives, seize upon details as an escape from fundamental responsibilities—they don't know what to do unless their desk is piled high with "work." Busy-ness, in the American scene, is often equated with importance.

Some find it difficult to delegate work. They may be cautious, unwilling to accept the work of others, or perfectionists who cannot see a job done less well than they themselves can do it. It used to be said of General MacArthur that he thought he could do everything better than everyone else and that the difficulty was that he could! Some presidents are fearful that if they delegate responsibility they have weakened their own positions. These are the inner problems of college presidents, and the way in which they solve such problems determines largely their administrative success.

Whether a college is large or small the areas of administrative concern for the president follow much the same pattern, for the pattern is dictated by what a college is and does. These broad categories are faculty, students, business, and public relations, the latter including alumni and athletic problems. With perhaps a little crowding almost everything can be got into these categories. The president may find himself personally more interested in one area than in others, although in the end he will have to accept responsibility for them all. Where he invests himself most may depend on particular urgencies which confront the college as well as upon his own inclinations and qualifications. Every president faces, at the outset, the problem of getting acquainted with the institution, with the alumni, and with whatever publics support it. Whether or not he enjoys public relations, he will be compelled to take a leading part in such activities because educational public relations has been claiming a steadily greater part of presidential time and energy. If he thrives on public occasions and discussion, as many college presidents do, this may be the area he reserves for his own special attention. If he prefers to avoid public addresses whenever he can, even though effective when he undertakes them, he may turn more of his attention to other administrative matters and delegate all that he can in the field of public relations. It will not be much.

The president finds himself at the head of an enterprise of the utmost variety. No matter how hard he works he cannot hope to be equally familiar with every phase. He must understand organization well enough to be able to invent appropriate procedures. Impulsive and *ad hoc* inventions are disturbing. Good organization requires thought and, once established, must be respected. Good organization requires a workable division of labor. If responsibility is to be accepted and carried out, clear and sufficient authority must be delegated. Relationships between people—the chain of command—must be well defined. Procedures must be invented which will require a minimum of red tape, but which will leave an intelligible record. For many reasons colleges are not distinguished for clarity and efficiency of organization. Yet the importance of good organization can hardly be overestimated. It reduces frustration, conserves time and energy. It will take a major part of the president's time and energy to devise organization, to adjust it to the qualifications of the people who must fit into it, and to unsnarl its inevitable kinks. His relation to some portions of it, and particularly to the philosophy which must guide him, deserves more extended discussion in chapters which follow.

As the head of a college, the president coordinates the work of others rather than doing detailed work himself. Suppose, for example, the college wants to buy a piece of land. It is not the president's duty to read the title description, or to substitute his appraisal of value for that of the superintendent of property, or to draft the terms of a mortgage, or even to determine the feasibility of the area as a future football field. But it is his duty to see that all of these things are done competently and promptly and that all information is supplied from any one administrator which will help each of the others to do his job. The president may, through his questions, actually become familiar with every part of the transaction, but if he takes over the responsibility for any single part of it he may well be substituting his judgment for a more expert one and, what may be even more serious, he will have relieved of responsibility those who should be expected to assume it. If the president is going to do over again the work of deans, directors, and superintendents, he will soon find himself swamped; he will also find that they no longer feel their former sense of responsibility for what he has taken over. Subordinates will make mistakes, but the mistakes will be fewer than those the president will make if he undertakes to do their work over again. If the president does not have competent assistants, it is his responsibility not to do their work himself but to find other assistants—itself sometimes the more distasteful and difcult task.

The president must delegate as much responsibility as possible and then respect the delegation. President Ernest Martin Hopkins of Dartmouth, one of the most effective college presidents of this generation, practiced the art of delegation perfectly. One of his board members said of him admiringly: "I'm sure he is a good president. He always appears to be sitting in the bleachers eating peanuts while the others are on the field playing the game."

Whether a president can be comfortable about leaving responsibility to others in part depends on whether they can or will accept it. This he can learn only by experience. In this respect college presidents are different from governors of states or the President of the United States. These officials appoint their own chief executive officers and assistants; a new college president, for the most part, works with those already chosen. Considering the high expectations with which colleges inaugurate new presidents, there should be a more realistic appreciation of the problems of the president who is trying to be effective through administrators who may not understand or be in sympathy with his program.

Virtually every college and university eventually is manned at all levels by administrators who have been long in office. In describing the problems of a president in establishing working relations with such a staff I do not for a moment wish to disparage the indispensable service such a staff performs. They are, for the most part, "career" people—registrars, admissions officers, accountants, assistants to deans, and others—who have literally given their lives to the institutions. Without their faithful and informed services the place would soon be chaos. The advent of a new president can be as difficult for them as they can be difficult for a new president. Fortunately, new presidents usually come into office with the best wishes of the staff. Where their knowledge and experience are placed willingly and cheerfully at his disposal the results are happy indeed. If then his judgment calls for changes to be made in fixed habits and practices, tact and patience are to be preferred to naked authority.

Frequently, however, a new president must work with deans, comptrollers, vice-presidents, property superintendents, who not only have been long in office but also have habits and loyalties adjusted to a different regime. A former president of a major Eastern university once said that when he assumed office he faced a formidable group of deans whom he decided to try to outlive rather than to remove, accepting in the meantime what he believed to be serious limitations on the progress the institution could make. Years later, he believed he had made the wrong decision.

This discussion raises one of the more difficult and unresolved problems of college administration—what to do about the tenure and status of vice-presidents, deans, and other administrative officers of corresponding rank, regardless of presidential changes. While nominally all administrative officers hold office "at the pleasure of the board of trustees," nevertheless they are not easily changed. If the officers are asked to resign, the resulting implication of incompetence or dissatisfaction is disastrous, both to them and to the president, as well as unpleasant for their friends and critics. Yet appointments for limited terms also have their drawbacks. Good scholars dislike to take up the burdens and anxieties of administrative work for a short time with resulting loss to their scholarly interests. Why lose time and momentum from their principal work of teaching and research? Furthermore, after a term as administrator or dean, a position as professorial colleague is difficult to resume both for him and for his associates. His associates feel too often that his years away from scholarship have taken their toll and the administrator in turn may find it difficult to overcome the barriers which were erected during the years of his administrative responsibilities. There are, incidentally, the matters of salary readjustments and of professional prestige. Administration imposes habits which often create occupational characteristics in those who hold such offices. They are not positions of final or primary authority, yet a strong dean, for example, frequently may be tempted to emphasize the importance of his position by adopting an independent attitude toward the president or an arbitrary one toward the faculty. Either creates trouble. Or, he may deliberately restrict himself to a narrow conception of his position and become virtually a clerical intermediary who accepts any recommendation and who receives and transmits any decision—without affecting either. The problem is a serious personal one for the parties at interest and for the administrative organization and leadership of higher education generally. It deserves a better solution than has been found.

The suggestion has sometimes been made that a new college or university president should, like a state governor, be permitted to name or bring with him his own cabinet of high administrative officers. The idea is more plausible than feasible. As a consequence, all such positions would share in the instability of presidential tenure. Such a plan would add greatly to the difficulty of recruiting good men in subordinate administrative positions. It would make the chief administrative officers a personal staff with more of a stake in the career of the president than in the welfare of the institution. It would sharpen the line between administrators as a group and others within the institution. It would reduce, for the institution, the value of experience in office accumulated over a period of years. The selection or removal of a president would become an impossible institutional decision if it always involved a decision to remove not only the president but also his cabinet.

These are formidable objections to a cabinet system in higher education. Yet in effect something approaching it actually exists. Sometimes a new president brings with him a trusted secretary or assistant. Frequently, provosts, vice-presidents, or deans may find it difficult or embarrassing to adjust to a new president and may, after an appropriate interval, ask for or be invited to accept a change of position or responsibility. The game of administrative musical chairs nearly always acquires increased tempo when there is a new director.

The indispensable instrument which a college president needs for good administration is information. He has a great deal to learn. Woodrow Wilson once observed that men cannot think without information, and the search for full, pertinent, accurate information must be a first care of every college president. If he does not have it, he will have to ask questions until he gets it or he will constantly run the danger of making uninformed and hence unwise decisions.

The range of information with which a college president must concern himself is enormous. It necessarily covers all the matters for which he has responsibility and this means virtually everything which affects the institution. Consider, for example, what he is required to know about students. In order to think about them competently he must know something about their number, where they come from, their quality, how they distribute themselves according to subjects and departments, the degree of their self-support, what they do after graduation, how many live in residences or at home, the coeducational balance, and any other facts he can get. Almost every question about college regulations, financial policies, faculty, building, or future planning will be related in some way to data about the students.

If anything, the president must be even more fully informed about the faculty. Even so, he will always feel himself insufficiently informed in order to make or review the delicate decisions about the faculty which relate to appointments, salary increases, promotions, separations, or arbitrations. Likewise, finance, with its kaleidoscopic changes and its relation to every phase of college operations, demands incessant study and thorough understanding. With all the possibilities of presidential errors which will always exist anyway, the president should make every effort to avoid those which might result from faulty or insufficient information.

The president must take the fullest care to see that information actually reaches him. It is no good to him unless he gets it. Every division of the college has its own form of organization and its own methods of reporting. Information about students, for example, may change significantly only at the end of a semester or even only at the end of the year; reports about them can be quite different and less frequent than, say, reports from the financial

THE PRESIDENT AS AN ADMINISTRATOR

office which the president may require on a monthly, quarterly, and annual basis. The president cannot gather such information for himself. He is dependent upon others, but he will save himself time and trouble if he himself thinks out clearly what kind of information he wants and what he wants to use it for, and explains this in turn to those who must get it for him. If he can tell them what he wants and what purposes it will serve, he will help his staff do a much more intelligent job and will give them a sense of significance about their work which will lift it above the routine.

While information is an elementary necessity for the administrator, for a variety of reasons it is not always easy to get. One of the reasons is that so much of the information that makes an institution work is carried around in peoples' heads, a part of their accumulated experience. Many of those who carry it are scarcely aware that it is there. If such information, however, is to be useful to a president, particularly a new one, it has to be got out of peoples' heads—reduced to writing or brought out in conference. Among all the people with memories or libraries in their heads, how is the president going to find out who knows what and how is he going to get from them what they know? Strangely enough, providing information for administrative use is not a highly developed academic activity, and a president with administrative experience may find himself with more than one member of his staff who does not actually know how to gather, organize, or put to use information which may be very significant. If it "hasn't been done that way before" a new president may become pretty weary before he can persuade people to try any other way.

There are several other obstacles which the president faces in getting information. The first is the colleague, administrator, or faculty member who is a practitioner of what I shall call the art of incomplete disclosure. This practice consists in disclosing only information which the informant, for reasons of his own, decides the president should have. The practitioner of this art ordinarily gives information which is scrupulously accurate, but it is never complete. For example, a recommendation for a proposed faculty appointment reaches the president's desk; everything is fully set down except, perhaps, the fact that the nominee is the son-in-law of the department head. Or a budget officer may present a picture of the budget which is most encouraging as compared to that of last year, but he neglects to say that the change is due primarily to the treatment this year of laboratory equipment as capital expenditure for future amortization rather than a charge against the current budget. I know a financial officer of a major university who under the tranquilizing effect of a few martinis remarked that his president "had never yet seen a complete financial report." The master of the art of incomplete disclosure is one of the most difficult of all administrative handicaps. He is always in a position to defend himself as to the truth of what he says and he can always claim innocence for what he did not say. Generally, when the whole story becomes known it is too late to rectify impressions which have been created or to modify decisions. So far as I know there is no cure for this foible. To deal with it the president must add to his administrative equipment an insatiable thirst for information and a sixth sense as to when he has obtained it, or he must be prepared to accept the consequences. It might be suggested, of course, that the president get rid of the offender, but the offense is rarely so clear or so overt as to justify such drastic action.

Speaking of human foibles as administrative problems, there are two others which the president will frequently encounter. One of these is the administrator who practices the art of the *fait accompli*—the thing having been done, what are you going to do about it? This practice takes such forms as overspending budgets; putting people on payrolls before their appointments have been officially approved; promising, in correspondence, things which

THE PRESIDENT AS AN ADMINISTRATOR

should never have been promised; or planning emergencies while the president is on vacation. It is a difficult administrative practice for the president to deal with for it usually requires an outright repudiation of the unauthorized act, imposing suffering upon innocent persons. The consequences of that are generally more serious than the acceptance of the act itself (the practitioners of the *fait accompli* seem to have a genius for judging this correctly). Repudiation too often involves damage to the credit or the integrity of the institution, repudiation of administrative aides, or the punishment of some innocent party. There are few sanctions which can be visited upon errant faculty or administrative personnel which are not too serious in fact to be invoked. About all the president can do to the practitioner of the *fait accompli* is to warn him "not to let it happen again," knowing all too well that if it does happen again he can't do much more than issue another warning. Only the most flagrant continuation or accumulation of offenses of this variety warrants dismissal.

One other complication for the president is the subordinate administrator who refuses to accept adequately his own proper responsibility. "Passing the buck" is the mark of the officeholder rather than the administrator. He transmits recommendations but he does not pass judgment on them. For example, a university may have only a limited amount of money for salary increases or be able to make only a few promotions. The buckpasser, however, passes along a full sheaf of recommendations—"let someone else decide." His first principle is self-protection. If the recommendations are approved he will be able to share or even to claim the credit; if not approved he cannot be blamed. This is one of the most difficult of all administrative practices to cure, as administrators in the army, big business, or government can testify. There is, in fact, only one cure—find persons of independent judgment who will accept responsibility, the responsibility their positions require.

Yet, even here, the president's example is crucial. If the president accepts *his* responsibility most of his associate administrators, except for the weak and incorrigible, will accept theirs. If the president continually greets the recommendations of deans, department heads, and committees with such phrases as: "all right, I'll go along" or "I won't object" or "if you want to, but—" his colleagues will quickly see no reason why their commitments should be any less reluctant or tentative than his. Recommendations which a president accepts become his as much as they are the recommendations of those who made them to him. If he tries to dissociate himself from such recommendations because they may turn out badly, he has only himself to blame if his colleagues follow his example.

After the president has set up a system for gathering all the information he can get, he is still faced by another great difficulty. This is the problem of compounding the truth out of what is laid before him. So much of the information a president receives is surrounded by a penumbra of interest, uncertainty, and incompleteness. The president must still find out what his information means. It is not that people deliberately attempt to mislead the president; it is rather that so many of the matters which are put before him are easily, even unconsciously, affected by the interests or associations of the reporter.

More subtle still is the fact that people are polite enough or politic enough to wish to give the president the answer they think he wants. "How good a teacher is Professor X?" A hint either way from the president as to why he inquires can get the desired answer—the evidence is never clear-cut. The problem of a president in asking for information is to avoid prejudicing the reply. By the time he extracts his own prejudices, preferences, and partisanship and those of his informants from any statement of fact, he needs all of his skill, intuition, and strength of character to determine its truth.

THE PRESIDENT AS AN ADMINISTRATOR

While the college president finds that getting information is one of his most difficult and essential administrative tasks, he also finds that giving information is one of his most useful administrative tools. There is no substitute for communication from a president as a means of giving a college or university a sense of unity. The president has or is believed to have more information about the institution as a whole than does anyone else. For him to share his knowledge with other administrators or with the faculty is reassuring. They like to think of themselves not as employees, but as partners in the enterprise. Nothing stimulates this feeling more than for the president to tell as much as he can of his hopes and his problems, of proposals he has laid before the board of trustees, and of the actions which the board takes. Secrecy is the enemy of confidence; to report as much as he can, as fully as he can, reduces uneasiness and suspicion, enlists interest, and may even generate help. Faculties, however, are smart, and reporting which is less than candid or sincere, or which omits essential elements, or is patronizing in attitude is rewarded with the contempt it will inspire. Indeed, it is likely to confirm a suspicion that something is being concealed. Where disclosure must be incomplete, or the limitation cannot be explained, silence is better.

Another general principle which the president finds immensely useful as effecting a sense of order and justice in his administration is respect for due process. Due process is not easy to define for the academic community, but it is essential. It is something more than an orderly way of doing things; it is the habit of giving an appropriate degree of consideration to the interests of all those who are directly concerned. In a complex university, a great number of people are concerned with almost anything which may be proposed. This is why as universities grow more complicated new programs and proposals are increasingly difficult to put into effect. (The older universities of the country find it generally easier to build an addition to the house than to do any remodeling.)

Suppose, for example, the College of Engineering wishes to introduce into its curriculum a requirement that its students should have an additional semester of English, a special brand called English for Engineers. Now begins the administrative "due process" by which a proper degree of consideration can be assured for the interests of all those who will be affected by such a proposal. Presumably, the instruction must be provided by the department of English, but that department is a part of the College of Arts and Sciences. Moreover, the English department does not see how it can provide additional sections or courses for engineers without a much larger staff, and, furthermore, it holds a strong educational conviction that engineers should be taught the same kind of English that is taught to everyone else. Engineering replies that their needs are different and if the English department is not willing to meet those needs sympathetically it will provide its own English teachers! In any event, what starts out as a simple proposal to remedy a deficiency in the education of engineering students quickly reveals itself as a matter of educational conviction and concern to two faculties, to several departments, and to the general university budget.

Of course, the question—a complex of educational, budgetary, and personal interests—has to be decided. A respect for due process sees to it that each interest has the opportunity to present its situation for consideration by a clear and swift procedure. This does not mean an endless wrangle of committees and administrators, but it does mean assurance that facts are presented, people and interests are given due consideration, and that the problem does get disposed of. Every effort must be made to work out compromises and to find areas of agreement. Nevertheless, the resulting decision will be distasteful to one or more of the several interests. But it would be far more distasteful, indeed demoraliz-

THE PRESIDENT AS AN ADMINISTRATOR 51

ing, if those who must finally yield feel that they have not been given consideration before judgment is rendered. Of course, a president can, if circumstances permit, employ salutary delay as one of his devices of management, but it is one to be employed with care.

Two more factors should be mentioned in connection with care for due process. The first is that it implies clear and careful organization, a constant subject of study for effective administration. Organization is not an exact science; organization is sometimes formal, sometimes informal. It will at different times involve standing committees, *ad hoc* committees, the observance of or sometimes the bypassing of established channels. The easy multiplication of committees and *ad hoc* machinery had better be fought—it will grow rapidly enough. Problems and processes that are recurrent, which will fit into a pattern, had better be kept within their regular channels. There will be more than enough exceptions and the regular, orderly procedures had better be observed.

A second important aspect of due process is that after it has been fairly observed it should result in decision. Too frequently presidents let debate go on indefinitely in the hope that eventually some consensus will emerge. What happens more often than not is that the debaters repeat themselves endlessly, retire to previously prepared positions, grow more skillful and determined in refuting each other, and settle down into their own version of the Greeks and Trojans. Such a war, unsettled, can drag out until the habit of fighting replaces the original battle over who is to get Helen. The "conference" as a device for the confrontation of parties at interest, presided over with clarity and good humor, is one of the president's most effective techniques.

Decisions which bring someone unhappiness or create anger are unpleasant and anyone who is human would prefer to avoid them. But the university president does well to learn early that, after reasonable respect for due process, indecision is far worse than unpleasant decisions. Clear and firm decision, like good surgery, creates the antiseptic conditions for healing; indecision allows infection to develop and spread unhindered. Nor are the strains and consequences of decision usually as unpleasant in fact as in anticipation. Uncertainty is paralyzing and most people would prefer even unfavorable knowledge to uncertainty. Decisiveness at least moves things ahead; an old situation, disposed of, is quickly superseded, even if not forgotten.

These are some of the problems and the obstacles which the conscientious administrator constantly encounters. They are intrusive, irritating, and negative. If they become his chief preoccupation, the enterprise gets nowhere. The problem of the administrator is to remember what administration is for, that it is not an end in itself, but always a means to an end. To help him meet some of the negative, irritating, and recurrent situations he needs a habit of cheerfulness and no small amount of personal courage. Above all, he must not let his own sensitivities or those of others make him tentative, procrastinating, and fearful. Charles Eliot once remarked that one of the necessary qualifications of a college president was an infinite capacity to inflict pain!

If, however, this were all there was to the college president's administrative work it would certainly be neither particularly distinctive nor worthwhile. As an administrator the president's real value is to impart to the management of the entire enterprise, by precept and even more by example, not the techniques but the *virtues* of good administration.

Discussions of administration are usually confined to technical matters, questions of proper methods, procedures, planning. The important elements of good administration, however, are not technical, but moral. No one has made this clearer than President Hutchins in his penetrating essay on the administrator.[1] The

[1] Robert M. Hutchins, "The Administrator," *Journal of Higher Education*, November 1946.

necessary virtues of administration, he said, are courage, fortitude, justice, and prudence or practical wisdom. To these President Eliot added patience as even more essential. At any rate, whether or not these exhaust the list it is clear that the successful administrator's qualifications must be more nearly those of character and intelligence than those of knowledge and experience.

In the practice of administration the college president encounters tests of all of these virtues every day. Some situations involve them all simultaneously—and perhaps a few others also. This is why administration is exhausting. Nor do the decisions have to be world-shaking; sometimes the smaller situations present the more subtle temptations. A president would never think of accepting a thousand dollars to admit a student to the medical school, but he may be tempted just to telephone casually to the chairman of the admissions committee to ask how the application of the son of his old friend is faring. Let the president of a college hint that friendship can affect a decision which should be based upon merit and he has given his tacit permission to every other administrator to take care of his friends.

This is why every decision of the president will be scrutinized for its moral qualities, to get some hint as to the factors which will be acceptable in the disposition of the work of the college. The president's example is the equivalent of a directive.

A college is a complex institution and its administrators may differ as much as faculty members as to the principal ends to be served and the best ways to serve them. Differences of opinion do not disappear on command; they yield only to persuasion. In this sense, the president is the most important teacher of the college. His classes are the students, the faculty, and his administrative colleagues; his subject is his philosophy of education and how the college must be administered in order to realize it. This is the distinctive job of the college president as an administrator.

IV

"Everything Takes Money"

Perhaps no change in higher education within recent years has been more apparent and more drastic than the growth of its housekeeping problems. The amounts of money and property now required for higher education, as I have already said, make it very big business. Large numbers of people with new and specialized skills have had to be added to staffs. Getting money, planning its wise expenditure, and administering the kinds of property now necessary for higher education have made demands on educators for skill and knowledge which they never had to possess before. To find such business qualifications in a president, combined with educational background and experience, is like discovering a diamond in a coal mine.

If Aesop were writing his fables today, he would not choose pouring water in a basket as a symbol of futility; he would choose a college president trying to find enough money for his institution. Harvard University or Mills College, or any other college for that matter, is always financially pinched. In 1957 Harvard's expenditures were approximately 50 million, Mills spent $1.25 million; but both are in need of more money—always! The disparity of millions in endowment and income makes no difference. Every college and university is *always* short of money. Their needs are measured by their aspirations and their aspirations know no bounds. As President Hutchins succinctly put it, a college or university which is not short of money has run out of ideas.

A more immediate factor to account for the shortage of funds in higher education is that few if any institutions can finance themselves on the basis of the tuition they charge. It is necessary to make up from other sources the difference between the cost of the student's education and what he pays. It is generally accepted in the United States that students should not pay the entire cost of their education, because we believe that there are general social values which society derives from the presence of educated people, and that it should contribute to the cost of producing them. Endowments and gifts for private and appropriations for public institutions are essential if education is to be cheap enough for young people to take advantage of it in the numbers our society requires. The line between the cost the student should bear, and that which should be borne by other sources, is drawn by economic conditions and by institutional needs.

There is much confusion on this point. In hammering home the view that students do not pay for more than, say, fifty per cent of the cost of their education, the colleges have failed to make clear that the costs of different kinds of education differ greatly and are very uneven. A small college with limited enrollment may, for many reasons, have a different student cost factor from a larger institution. Graduate and professional schools and research activities are particularly expensive forms of specialized education, yet these expenses are usually included in the generalized estimates universities make as to how much it costs to educate a student. It may, for example, cost $20,000 to educate a student for four years in a medical school, of which the student himself may actually pay not more than ten per cent. In some universities as much as one-fourth to one-third of the entire budget may be spent on the medical school with perhaps not more than three or four hundred students involved. In the same institution, however, a student in undergraduate courses in the liberal arts may pay every cent of what can be attributed legitimately to the costs of his education. Indeed, his tuition fees may not only pay the full costs of his own education, they may help importantly to pay for other institutional costs which are related only distantly, if at all, to his personal educational benefits. More candor and better cost accounting would be beneficial to all concerned.

If colleges and universities are by their nature always short of funds, the college president who gets this principle firmly in mind will save himself some psychological problems. It will help him, for example, to accept the fact that he is on a treadmill. He is destined always to approach but never to arrive at the promised land. He may be as successful with donors as was President Hopkins at Dartmouth or with legislatures as was President Sproul of California—nevertheless the horizon merely recedes. Nor should the president ever expect gratitude from the college for the money he gets. This he is expected to do. No matter how successful he may be there are few laurels with dollar marks on them for him. While he may ease the strains of his office by being a good provider, he can never hope to make it comfortable. New levels of expenditure are quickly accepted; salary increases are regarded merely as justice, usually overdue, and a new building provided for chemistry makes, by contrast, biology's need still more glaring.

In discussions of financing higher education, it is customary to assume that there are differences between public and private institutions, educationally and financially, which are traceable to their respective sources of support. It is usually said that private institutions are freer from unwelcome influence or control than are publicly supported colleges and universities. In my own opinion, the differences are less than are usually supposed. Actually the source of support is not so important as is the fact that additional money must be raised. So long as additional money is necessary the donor—private philanthropist or public agency—must be cultivated. (While the effects on institutional policy of this financial dependence are basically the same for both public and private institutions, they are more readily seen in the former than in the latter. If, for example, a state university seeks to add a half million dollars to its income by increasing student fees, the legislature which provides the supplementary appropriations is always tempted to cut these appropriations by a corresponding amount. If a public institution tries to build up endowment funds or other independent sources of support, unless they can be earmarked for highly specialized purposes, it encounters the same difficulty. In short, whatever source—public or private—provides or can withhold the marginal income an institution finds essential is in a position to exert great influence upon it.) All colleges and universities must have money over and beyond the amounts they collect as tuition and incidental fees. The *need* for this money, not its *source*, creates the temptation common to both public and private institutions to please those who hold their fates in their hands. If the public institution is self-conscious as to the effect of its activities on legislatures, the private institution is equally apprehensive of its relations to alumni and prospective donors. While Harvard, Yale, Chicago, and Princeton may achieve sufficient independence to be able to ignore the criticisms and protests of particular individuals, no matter how wealthy or influential, there are also state institutions which successfully maintain themselves beyond overt political control. Of that large number of institutions, both public and private, which do tremble by reason of their precarious financial support, I doubt if there is much difference in the degree or kind of concern or of accommodation which each will reveal when its bread and butter is threatened.

Actually, there is little to choose between the job of the president who must lobby with or placate a legislature and the president who must cultivate private donors. The one must avoid too much political compromise, and the other must resist the attachment of humiliating or fatal strings to private benefactions.

Of the two, my sympathies are with the presidents of private institutions as having the more difficult job. Not only is it harder now to get private money in sufficient amounts, despite foundations and corporate gifts, but the problem of dealing with the desire on the part of individual donors to control or influence institutions is more difficult. Usually, people who have made enough money to give some away have strong ideas as to what they would like done with it. If they do not give it for some specific purpose which may have a distorting effect upon the well-rounded development of an institution, they may attach bizarre or whimsical conditions which, if not actually harmful, can be humiliating.[1] If a legislature attaches unusual conditions for appropriations, those conditions must at least be agreed to openly and by a considerable number of people. The matter is open to public scrutiny. Furthermore, the president of the public institution can say to a legislature, "This university belongs to the public, and it is your *duty* to support it." The president of the private university has no such lever; his appeal must be to a more complex set of interests—duty, perhaps, and a sense of public service, but more frequently to sheer generosity, institutional pride, and loyalty, sentimentality, or even vanity.

The need for money is education's Old Man of the Sea, and most of the time he will sit squarely on the shoulders of the president, no matter how much help the latter may enlist to assist him with the load. No matter how he tries to organize himself or his institution, the college president cannot fully escape the money-

---

[1] Illustrations of the whimsical interests of private donors are numerous. One of the more recent was that of the citizen who gave a large sum of money to Johns Hopkins University provided the university would have painted upon its walls a mural of the ten loveliest belles of Baltimore who were prominent during the donor's youth.

"EVERYTHING TAKES MONEY"

raising job. "To beg like a college president" has become a well-understood simile. People who appropriate or give money want to deal with principals, not agents, and this means the president.

Fund raising has become so important and such a proportionately large part of institutional activities that in most institutions, regardless of size, it is now given special organization. Professional fund raising corporations have entered the field; cooperative organizations have been formed, particularly among private schools, to seek funds collectively; educational campaigns to stimulate gifts from corporations have been developed, and alumni appeals and special drives are continuous. Such money-raising activities require special machinery—a development office, an alumni organization, or similar devices. Public relations and information offices carry their share of the load and in public institutions someone is usually detailed to follow closely any political developments which may affect institutional interests.[2]

With his money in hand or in prospect, the next job of the president is to see that its expenditure is prudently planned. In the annual or biennial budget, the college president meets all his problems at once. In every allocation of funds, he is deciding institutional and educational destiny. Since there is never enough money, to say "yes" to one request is to say "no" to a half dozen others. The conscientious college president must try to know something about what he is not approving, as well as what he is approving, if he is to choose wisely among the possibilities before him and if the ghosts of slain proposals are not to return to haunt him.

Fortunately, budget making in practice is less dramatic than such a statement implies. Colleges and universities are already going concerns and most of their funds are firmly committed

[2] I remember hearing the president of Notre Dame say with a sigh that he had to raise four million dollars a year just to balance Notre Dame's annual budget! Other presidents sigh more or less deeply. The final responsibility is for the president inescapably personal.

long before annual budgets are discussed—so much so that many a president thinks plaintively that all his decisions are made for him before he is even asked for them. (Let no president think for a minute that the coal money can be taken to increase the pay of the professor of history!) The strain of budget making comes in allocating annually the small but crucial discretionary funds. It is only here that the college, financially speaking, can be different this year from last, or next year from this one.

Colleges are gyroscopically controlled enterprises. Their directions and speed are set and sudden changes, while unlikely, are almost sure to be catastrophic. Colleges yield only to continuous pressures persistently applied, and the comparatively small amounts of money in the budget about which genuine choices can be made provide a president with one of his most valuable means of exerting pressure. In any college or university, virtually ninety per cent of the budget for the next year will be like the budget for the past year, spent for the same purposes, paid to the same people and in approximately the same amounts. Ten per cent can be different: there are some deaths and resignations, some new money from gifts, appropriations, or other income, or there is occasionally an unexpected saving. This is the area where the choices are all-important. For example, suppose there is some additional money which can be spent for the department of English (whether $50,000 at California or $2000 at William and Mary, the educational problem is the same). How shall it be invested? Of the various kinds of work carried on in the department, what should be most encouraged or rewarded? With the retirement of Professor Swinburne, should another eminent scholar be brought in as a full professor, or should the department be rebuilt from below? Is this the year to equip a dramatic workshop? What about the creative writing courses? Or a poet in residence? The cloth must be measured seven times; it can be cut but once. The

"EVERYTHING TAKES MONEY"

same process must, to some degree, go on in every department where a choice of expenditures is possible.

Above the departmental level, the choices are even more crucial and difficult. Is what they are saying true about mathematics, and that the college will have to break the general faculty salary scale in order to secure or to hold its mathematicians—or physicists, or pathologists? And if we don't devote every spare cent to the new physics equipment, might we not as well forget our chances to compete in an indispensable field? Is the bull market in psychology over, or must we push romance languages out of their floor in order to expand the psychology laboratory?

The choices have to be made, and unfortunately a good bit of human frailty as well as institutional compulsion creeps into their making. The valuable faculty member gets an offer from another institution and must be kept—no choice there. The squeaky wheel will, in another year, become unbearable, unless given a little grease; inequities must be rectified in the salaries of the art department; and deferred maintenance refuses to be deferred any longer. Something must be done for the women's gymnasium to prove that the college is really interested in its girls. Thus the domain of purely educational choice grows smaller and smaller.

Making up the budget of a college or university is in itself an educational process, and while the president will get most of the education, he shouldn't get it all. Properly used, both the making and the administration of a budget are among the most useful administrative instrumentalities a president has for developing a sense of responsibility not only among the administrators of the college, but in the faculty as well. Making the budget involves choices and decisions and the president should get others to help make them. If people are involved in decisions, they will be more inclined not only to accept them but also to defend and to take responsibility for them. The budget provides such an opportunity. Even if the knowledge of individual salaries must be confined as restricted information to the small number of administrators who must know them, the general resources of the college should be freely discussed with everyone who would be helped by such knowledge, certainly with deans, relevant administrative staff, and department heads. All of these need to know where the college gets its money, how much it gets, what the demands of fixed overhead amount to, what its urgent building needs are, and some of its financial prospects. People think more reasonably when they have information on which to base their judgments. Such information gives everyone concerned a greater sense of partnership, and helps to dissipate the shadows of suspicion which secrecy casts. One of the common faults of administrators is their reluctance to discuss even general information widely. Apparently they fear that sharing information also means sharing power, or that their decisions will be more easily subjected to attack. Every administrator should remember that he is not a proprietor but a transient trustee; no college, private or public, belongs to those who temporarily run it.

If others are invited to help the president make up a budget, they will find it necessary to do the same kinds of agonizing which all budget makers are compelled to do. If all the decisions are made by a president, a central budget officer, or by the deans, such officers will, by that fact, be compelled to take undivided responsibility for these decisions. Under such a system a department head can quite justly say to his colleagues: "I recommended both a salary increase and a promotion for you, but 'they' wouldn't allow it." Suppose, however, the department head is told: "All the budget estimates together run $600,000 beyond any income the college can hope to have next year. This means your recommendations will have to be cut by ten per cent. Will you please indicate how you think this should be done, keeping in mind the best interests, present and future, of the department as a whole?" Such a step enlists the responsible help of the person

"EVERYTHING TAKES MONEY"

most intimately acquainted with the department's work. The department head must think over the program again and he must now defend his recommendations to others. It is a sobering experience. He must decide whether for this duty he is a foreman or a member of the union—in the language of business, "a company man or a customer's man." Of course, recommendations must still be reviewed by superior, more general and even more impersonal authority, for department heads are themselves frequently too much involved personally in departmental matters to retain their perspective. Recommendations must be reviewed with wider institutional considerations in mind, but the collective judgment resulting from participation in budget making will make better decisions.

While the president can use the making and administration of a budget as a useful educational instrument, he can also use it as a lethal one. "There isn't enough money" can be a president's most effective answer to any proposition he doesn't like. In a way it is always true—there never *is* enough money. This can be his shortest answer, and also his most shortsighted. Theoretically, the merits of an educational proposal are never dependent on whether there is money; if the proposal is a good one, there is a moral obligation on the administrator to try to get the money. If a president staves off pressure by the easy budgetary reply of "no money," he will soon find that he is killing off the fertile ideas of those who build institutions. A wise president, no matter how harried, never makes the budget an educational guillotine.

The problems of business management have in the last few years mushroomed faster than any other phase of college and university operation. The sums of money involved are greater; the numbers of students, faculty, administrative staff, and service employees have grown; more property is required; new governmental relationships, contracts, and regulations have sprouted; and student "accounting"—registration, credits, reports—has multiplied.

With this huge increase in housekeeping, two college officers have acquired vastly greater importance: the business manager and the superintendent of property. Good men in these positions are above price and can be among the most helpful staff members an institution can have; inadequate ones, among its most fruitful sources of trouble. The normal instinct of men trained in the management of business and property is to think of their responsibilities in terms of income, expenditures, costs, accounting, balanced budgets, and operating efficiency. To many of them education is excruciatingly unbusinesslike, and they feel it their duty "to bring it into line." Tension can run high between the strictly business and the academic points of view.

This is the president's educational opportunity. With tact and patience he may succeed not only in convincing the business management that all the property and all the expenditures are for the purpose of "producing education"; he may induce them to consider some new criteria. He may get them to see that they all fail, faculty and business management alike, unless they do "produce education"—balanced budgets and beautiful grounds notwithstanding. So armed, a superintendent of property can eventually listen without shuddering to the water running all night in a laboratory, and the business manager can watch without heightened blood pressure the lights blazing in the library when only a few students are there.

One of the discoveries which gives presidents and other thoughtful students of higher education some long thoughts is the large and ever-increasing amount of college and university resources which go into everything but the teaching and research which are generally thought of as "education."

Administrative overhead is taking a larger bite out of every college dollar regardless of the size of the college or of the number of dollars. While college accounting is still far from being a science, there is general agreement that at least half of all expendi-

"EVERYTHING TAKES MONEY" 65

tures fall in nonacademic categories. One of the largest universities in the Middle West believes, in moments of privacy and candor, that not more than thirty-five cents out of each of its dollars goes into strictly academic operations. The phenomenon is worrisome, but explainable. Wages for nonacademic help—janitors, elevator operators, heating plant engineers, groundsmen, watchmen, secretaries, bookkeepers, clerks, cooks, and residence hall operators—have risen over the decade more rapidly than academic salaries. Furthermore, the numbers of the nonacademic staff have increased, with new college and university public services, with increased records to be kept and accounting of every kind (just consider the monthly payroll problem with its variety of income tax, social security, hospitalization, workmen's compensation, and other withholding operations), and with the addition of all manner of new activities. The fringe benefits, gradually extending throughout our society, of health and life insurance, pensions, and paid vacations, now cover the entire university staff. The five-day week of the nonacademic staff more than any other factor has eliminated Saturday classes on most campuses. However desirable these developments may be from many social points of view, they are financially costly and go far to explain why college business managers are beside themselves to make clear (even to some of their presidents!) why nonacademic costs rise even more steeply than do the academic.

Moreover, everything a college buys has gone up in price. Inflation is the mortal enemy of nonprofit institutions which cannot pass along their increased costs to an ultimate customer. And the capital investment in classroom and laboratory buildings, in dormitories, and in their equipment, has soared, with consequent increases in interest payments and maintenance charges.

These economic shifts are to be seen in no place more clearly than in the management of the property of the colleges and universities. American colleges, in an earlier era of cheap land and cheap labor, went in heavily for fine buildings and park-like campuses. Pleasant as these are, they now entail huge capital investments and constantly growing maintenance costs. The same economic forces which have boarded up the estates of Newport society and pulled down Fifth Avenue town houses, which have transformed hotel rooms into good-sized telephone booths and hastened the development of automation, are now at work on the colleges. A recent statement by President Pusey that Harvard needs forty million dollars to meet its current building needs is at once an index of new costs and a warning that some new ideas about educational facilities and their management would be warmly welcomed.

Let no president be misled—the demands of property upon the budget may be less articulate than those of the faculty and staff, but they are more relentless. All those ivied halls have windows, roofs, heat-lines, and sewer systems, and their demand for attention, paint, and repair, especially in emergencies, can exceed any human insistence. Maintenance deferred is nearly always maintenance doubled. A broken window may cost five dollars to repair; left unrepaired the attendant damage can amount to hundreds. "Everything takes money."

Yet professors are not guiltless of contributing to higher costs of college education. They must carry particular responsibility on two counts. The first is in an insistence on equipment and facilities which may be of doubtful necessity and which are infrequently or inefficiently used. At the risk of decapitation, I suggest that one compare the austerity of the physics, chemistry, or biology laboratory of, say, a British university with an American college and then ask whether the costs of our equipment can be reflected in the superiority of student or faculty work. Any spirit of asceticism or even of self-restraint among, for example, our college scientists has suffered erosion under the generosity of government surplus property and contract research and the gifts or salesmanship of industry. Competition among colleges also plays its part; keeping up with the Joneses requires that "if the department at Michigan has two electron microscopes we must have two." Likewise, professorial proprietorship makes for inefficient use. Many a professor would rather share his toothbrush than his laboratory.

The second area of faculty responsibility is in the curriculum, the multiplication of courses. Knowledge, to be sure, is steadily growing, but the apparent belief that it all must be taught and taught in new courses is ridiculous. A university with six hundred courses in professional education has merely insured that no one will ever have much knowledge of the field—life isn't that long. A department of English which believes it must have a separate seminar on every prominent author has forgotten the purpose of seminars. The curriculum of higher education needs the guidance of educational philosophy.

Too often, additions to the curriculum have had no other educational sanctions than the desire of the professor to "give a course" on his currently favored topic. The inclusion of new courses has added many valuable things to curricula which should, of course, have been added, but the uncontrolled expansion has also threatened the possibility of putting together a general education from the patchwork of courses—and it has added very substantially to college costs. These are high prices for this particular form of academic freedom.[3]

This lack of institutional self-control would, at first glance, appear to be nothing more than poor administration. Actually the reasons for it lie much deeper. They stem from the diversity and individuality of the American system (some would prefer to say anarchy) of higher education which makes every college and

[3] I have discussed this topic much more fully in "The Flowering Curricula of American Higher Education," *Annals of the American Academy of Political and Social Science*, September 1955, p. 58.

university a rival of some, if not all, others. They are in competition for money, students (numbers or quality), faculty, facilities, and prestige. Why, then, should an institution deliberately impose upon itself limitations which might handicap it in its efforts to meet its competition? If one college or university finds for itself a point of unusual distinction—a seminar for space study, a center for Oriental art, a poet in residence, a rewarding research contract—its rivals must duplicate it or find an equivalent of their own. It is this necessity which largely explains why the curriculum proliferates, why there is so much institutional duplication, and why efforts at joint planning and cooperation are so few and feeble.[4]

While the habits of mind of a free enterprise society have been carried into academic life farther than they should have been, competition in higher education is not all bad. If the alternative to it is some form of central planning and control, most of us would have no trouble making up our minds as to which we would prefer. The point is that the colleges and universities, as a part of the price of their complete freedom, diffuse their energies and resources in competition which leaves them little opportunity to improve their own status through devices of better management. As in most instances of sharp competition, the beneficiaries (if any) are the "customers," not the competitors—the students and public, not the colleges themselves.

Turning to a different aspect of finance in American higher

[4] In a number of states the rivalry between some public institutions has become so sharp that it has divided legislators and citizens into highly partisan groups. Educational progress under such circumstances might be described as "double or nothing," i.e., either all the rival institutions must be treated equally well or all equally neglected.

Veblen, *The Higher Learning in America* (New York: Huebsch Co., 1918), 89 ff., has some interesting observations on institutional rivalry, why it exists, and some of its consequences. He holds that it is a consequence of the habits of thought induced by business and "uncritically carried over into academic affairs"—an explanation too meager to account for the phenomena.

education, the art (I refuse to call it a science) of cost accounting has got almost nowhere. This is one of the most baffling facts a board of trustees encounters. As businessmen, most of them cannot understand it. The reason is that education is largely an investment in faith: we know what it costs, but we do not know what it is worth. Education is by nature a low-efficiency operation; we don't know, when we spend our money, how much we ought to spend, how much we are going to get for our money, or how we might get more. Who knows, for example, what a course in art, in English literature, or in mechanical engineering is worth? Is it worth more if it is taught to fifty rather than to ten students? Suppose a Nobel or Pulitzer prize winner is among the ten? The cost accountant can chase but he can never capture this elusive value element in education.[5]

Nevertheless, it would be better for themselves if colleges and universities would take a little harder look at some of their management practices. It may be impossible to answer the question as to how much an education is worth or how much should be paid for it. But this is no reason why, with any given staff, student body, and facilities, common sense should not apply. If society is willing to support people who study words, dig up artifacts, experiment with apparatus, or even spend most of their lives talking in the belief that enduring values will emerge, the people who are supported ought not to suffuse their activities with any carelessness, vagueness, or self-indulgence that can be prevented. Educators ought to see the inherent uncertainty and in-

---

[5] How this characteristic of educational expenditures exasperates business managers is reflected in Harry L. Wells, *Higher Education Is Serious Business* (New York: Harper & Brothers, 1953). One quotation will suffice: "Some day a confident cost accountant is going to be elected president of a university, and the prejudices and traditions which retard the application of cost control in our field will be broken down," p. 6. His comments on space utilization in colleges are withering—with such methods, he says, no commercial enterprise could survive.

efficiency of their art not as an excuse for complacency but as a challenge to prove its worth.

Schedules, curricula, the use of buildings and facilities, could all yield to better management in many a college and university. Why they do not is a long story. Tradition, habit, academic freedom, and sheer irresponsibility are intermingled. Students who are employed part-time; professors with strong proprietary instincts over classrooms, laboratories, books, and equipment; students and professors with aversions to classes before nine or after three; automobiles and long weekends; these are a few of the obstacles to better management. I know many campuses where a gunshot in the middle of the afternoon would not only hit no one: there would scarcely be anyone about to hear it.

A few years ago, one president discovered that some eighty per cent of all the classes in the university were held in the forenoon. Knowing the pressure on space and the demand for new buildings, he urged a better distribution. He said it was hardly fair to ask the legislature for more buildings, unless the university made better use of the ones it had. After a year of urging, he found that he had succeeded in getting the proportion of morning classes reduced from eighty to seventy-eight per cent.

Better management the colleges need and ought to have. At the risk of showing my own sympathies, I will say, however, that I hope that the invasion of the campuses by cost accounting, efficiency experts can be stopped short of complete occupation. Infiltration I should be glad to see, but the important elements of education—inspiration, experimentation, originality—will not thrive in an atmosphere of factory production. There are "inefficiencies" the public will have to accept if it wants the *best* kind of education. If the experts ever succeed in making higher education efficient, it will be more inefficient than it is now! The cost accounting kind of mind will never be happy with higher education.

V

Presidents and Boards of Trustees

ALMOST every institution of higher education in the United States, whether public or private, is a corporation whose powers are created and specified by law. These powers are usually vested, under the legislative act or charter which creates the corporation, in a board of trustees which owns property, enters into contracts, accepts responsibility for the acts of its officers and employees, and provides the institution with its continuity. No one can understand American higher education until he knows something of the way in which such boards are constituted and how they exercise their powers.[1]

To the faculty and to most of the administrators of colleges and universities, the board of trustees is a distant and mysterious body which, although meeting only occasionally, exercises a powerful but subtle and pervasive influence on the institution. Except in the case of the president, there is usually little contact or

[1] An excellent discussion of boards of trustees is to be found in a report recently published: "The Role of the Trustees of Columbia University" (New York: Columbia University, 1958).

acquaintance between the members of the board of trustees and members of the faculty or administrative staff. The trustees visit the campus for occasional meetings; their business is not a matter of common knowledge, and the limited contact which there is with the college personnel is characterized by the usual formulae of friendly interest which effectively serve to block genuine communication, especially on important matters. This sense of distance is natural and inevitable. Faculty and staff come and go, as do trustees, and there is little necessity for either personally to know the other. The trustees are usually nonresidents; their vocational interests and social circles are different from those of the faculty; and, indeed, the relationship which each bears to the institution precludes any common basis for an association between faculties and boards which could be called normal.

Let no one be misled, however. The apparently slight and legalistic relationship between the board of trustees and the people who daily operate a college is not the measure of their influence upon each other. The board of trustees is a brooding force, present in spirit even when not present in body, frequently exerting influence informally more effectively than by formal resolutions. And boards, in their turn, are vaguely aware that faculties differ from themselves in their interests and preoccupations, that they hold almost unpredictable views about what things are important, and that they must be handled with care and sometimes indulged in seemingly strange vagaries.

In addition to their legal and proprietary services, boards of trustees provide for education another service which has been found salutary for many other institutions in our society, namely, the union of laymen and experts. Such unions are too well accepted in the United States to require justification here, but the values are nowhere more apparent than in education. Education is not an exact science. Its experts can profit from the criticisms and suggestions of intelligent laymen and from the necessity, as experts, to describe their activities and to formulate their own views clearly and convincingly. Lay boards can help presidents and faculties to interpret education. They can ward off misunderstandings and shield institutions from attacks. Their presence as laymen is reassuring to less well-informed constituents and publics.

If, in the pages which follow, there appear to be criticisms of boards and of board members, such criticisms should not be regarded as an attack on the principle of the lay board, but rather of particular individuals and practices. Higher education as a whole and certain colleges and universities in particular have reason to be grateful for the generosity and public spirit of the many intelligent citizens who serve as trustees.

How are such boards constituted, and what kinds of persons compose them? There is no common pattern of size, selection, or membership among American colleges and universities. In private schools, the number of trustees, their mode of selection, and terms of office are usually laid down in the college charter. Ordinarily such boards are self-perpetuating, that is, they select their own successors and fill their own vacancies. For better or worse, this naturally means perpetuation in their own image. The board may be small (Harvard has only seven members), or it may be large (Cornell has forty-five). To speak of an average would be meaningless. Church-related colleges sometimes have *ex officio* representation from the church, and alumni representation is now frequently provided on the boards of both public and private institutions.

There is even greater variety in the size and composition of the boards of public institutions. State universities are almost equally divided between those whose boards are elected by popular vote and those whose boards are appointed, usually by the governor. Other state colleges, such as teachers colleges, are usually governed by state boards of education, which have broad and general educational jurisdiction. To reduce in public institutions the possibilities of transitory political influence or control, the terms of board members are sometimes made long—fourteen years, for example, at Louisiana State University, seventeen years at the University of California—or are sometimes staggered, so that no governor is likely to appoint a majority of the board during his own, or at least a single, term of office. Sometimes a governor is also limited in making his appointments by the requirement of legislative confirmation or by the necessity to appoint members from more than one political party. Where members are elected by popular vote, the office is in some cases nonpartisan, or the number to be elected from any one party may be limited.

What kinds of people are to be found on college or university boards of trustees? The position itself helps to determine such memberships. Trusteeships take time. They are usually unpaid; hence they are likely to be held by those who have some command of their time and who can afford them. These facts alone give the job the distinction of unselfish service and of social prestige.

The boards of private colleges have the power to determine their own composition. Since they are self-perpetuating, they are likely to be very homogeneous in membership. Members may be selected for their social prominence, or their political importance, as well as the possibility of some particular service (philanthropy, for example) which they can perform for the institution. Usually such persons are selected because of a known habit or a record of public service. Hence the high percentage of wealthy, successful, and public-spirited men and women on college boards. Membership on the boards of public institutions, while not so obviously related to personal success or wealth, nevertheless reflects many similar factors of political indebtedness, ambition, personal reputation, or a strong desire for public service. The governors of several states have told me that no positions within their gift create more pressure for appointments than do memberships on the boards of trustees of their state universities.[2]

[2] One generalization can be offered about boards of trustees to which

By and large, the members of the boards which control higher education, whether public or private, are drawn from the ranks of the more successful businessmen, lawyers, and professional people. Among land-grant colleges, farmers have received some representation. In recent years labor has demanded and received (at Cornell and California, for example) representation.[3] This identification of trustees with the conservative elements of the community has been the subject of some of the most acid criticisms from commentators on higher education. Perhaps the most famous of these is Upton Sinclair's *The Goosestep*, which charged that higher education was controlled by the same men who controlled big business. While Sinclair showed conclusively that many of the men who sat on the boards of directors of large corporations were also members of the boards of trustees of many colleges and universities, he was less convincing in showing that these men exercised an unduly repressive influence on higher education. Sinclair believed that there was an intent on the part of big business to control education in its own interests and to make it an instrument of its own propaganda. Undoubtedly some of the original founders in the early days of particular institutions did exercise a degree of control incompatible with academic freedom —thus at Clark University, where Jonas Gilman Clark, and at Stanford, where Senator and Mrs. Stanford made the lives of presidents and faculties miserable through their personal interventions in university affairs. On the other hand, these can be countered with the liberalism of John D. Rockefeller at the Uni-

---

numerous and justifiable exceptions will be taken. It is that, as a whole, the trustees of public institutions take their responsibilities more seriously than do those of private institutions. The reasons for this are that the records of public institutions, including the actions and attendance of trustees, are subject to public scrutiny, thus establishing a higher degree of individual accountability. Furthermore, terms of service are more frequently specified and limited on public than on private boards, and there are fewer purely "honorary" appointments.

[3] Earl McGrath, "The Control of Higher Education in America," *Educational Record*, XVII, April 1936, p. 264.

versity of Chicago and the statesmanship of Johns Hopkins in founding the Johns Hopkins University; both accorded the institutions complete freedom for self development.

While it can scarcely be shown that the conservative elements of the community conspire to control higher education, it is clear that most boards of trustees reflect their views. Chosen from conservative, influential professional and business men, whose success is identified with the *status quo*, it is not surprising that boards of trustees should naturally believe that preservation of the *status quo* is a highly desirable service, whether performed by institutions of higher education or by other institutions. The influence of such men upon higher education is not the overt, intentional thing which Sinclair believed; it arises, rather, from the transmission through university administrators of the conservative views which such men hold. Admittedly this can be an unseemly, dictatorial insistence that such views pervade the institution; actually, the prevalence of conservative policies results more frequently from the coincidence of views which board members and college administrators hold in common. Is it surprising that administrators chosen by boards should share the basic views and attitudes of those boards?

It should be said, however, that with the revolution which in recent years has overtaken American business—a revolution which has greatly broadened the conception of its responsibility—boards of trustees reflect a somewhat more appropriate view of the services they must perform.[4]

In its relationship to the college and in the discharge of its own responsibilities, a board operates almost exclusively through the president. He is the source of its information. He is the agent

[4] The "control" of higher education in the United States is a subject which can generate high blood pressure among debaters both on and off the campus. For a thoughtful but much more critical point of view than that expressed here, see Robert S. Lynd, "Who Calls the Tune," *Journal of Higher Education*, April 1948, p. 163.

whom it must hold responsible. This is the most important fact in understanding the position of the college president and the parts which both he and the board play in the administration of the institution. In this relationship, most of the effectiveness and most of the difficulty between presidents and boards are to be found.

That the president is virtually the sole or at least the responsible means of communication between the board and the rest of the institution is administratively sound, if for no other reason than that any other system is worse. If a board establishes independently of the president either formal or informal pipelines between itself and members of a college staff, it will find itself completely bewildered by the flood of fact, tale-bearing, complaints, suggestions, and rumors it has invited. It will make itself the recipient of diverse plans, critical reports, special pleas, and ill-conceived suggestions which can bring it only confusion or impose on it or the president endless explanations.

For a board to give to subordinate administrative officers independent access to it or to seek information except through the president are sure ways to undermine the administrative authority of the president and, ultimately, the board's confidence in him. Nothing will make an institution quiver to its foundations more quickly than evidence or rumor that the board relies more confidently upon someone else than it relies upon the president. Let the board question the president all it pleases; let it direct him to supply more information or to give the matter more study. Let it even flatly disagree with him and reject his proposals on the merits he claims for them; but let it not seek, without the president's knowledge or arrangement, direct contact with other officers or with faculty members, thus implying doubts as to his honesty or adequacy—unless, of course, it wishes to destroy him.

This Janus-like relationship of the president to a board of trustees on the one hand and to the faculty and staff on the other imposes upon him a complicated and sobering responsibility. The board must rely upon him for the information upon which it must act intelligently. As sophisticated men of experience, they are usually shrewd enough to know when such information is complete and whether it is reliable—it is their responsibility to ask questions. If the president is careless about staff work, if his reports are shoddy, if he bluffs or practices the art of incomplete disclosure, the board sooner or later is sure to find it out, and his every report will be viewed with suspicion thereafter. A president who tries to "make an impression" on a board will succeed: the impression will be that of a man trying to make an impression.

Except as the board may request, it is largely up to the president to decide what the board shall hear. But he must place before it all information and all views which he thinks the board may regard as pertinent, whether they are his views or not. It rests upon him to develop understanding between the staff of an institution not directly represented to the board, and a board not in direct communication with the staff. The chances for mischief or misunderstanding are numerous. The safeguard lies in the good sense and integrity of board members and the president, and in the degree of their mutual confidence.

While this principle of the unique relationship between a board and a president is sound, its rigidity is, in practice, frequently modified. Some presidents are intensely jealous of their liaison position between the board and the staff and make no secret of their displeasure over any lapses into direct communications. Although a president cannot control the curiosity of a trustee or his freedom of speech, he can let his wrath fall upon any subordinate who talks. Other presidents are more relaxed in the matter. Some introduce subordinate officers or faculty members into meetings of the board or its committees, knowing the advantages to the board of occasionally hearing those who are most deeply and directly involved in the matters before them, while at the same time reassuring the staff that the full merit of their case has been stated because they themselves had the privilege of stating it. Good sense and good manners must rule. If, on such occasions, the members of the board discover and seek to develop a difference of opinion between the president and his staff on matters presented to them, nothing but mutual embarrassment can come from the discussion.

In some institutions, faculty committees have been set up to establish direct relationships between boards and faculties in order to supplement the communication between them, or to reduce their mutual dependence upon the president as their sole liaison contact. For the most part, these arrangements have not proved successful. The implications as to their mutual faith in the integrity or the efficiency of the president is a little too bald for either group to be comfortable in the presence of the other. Where such relations have been established, as, for example, at the University of Wisconsin, they usually settle down into mere social occasions, and not very pleasant ones at that because of the necessity on the part of all concerned to talk about nothing important. The suggestion that faculties should also have members on boards has found even less favor. For faculty members to sit as members of a board of trustees involves too many situations in which there is a conflict of interest.[5]

[5] In this connection some comments of Ordway Tead, a former chairman of the Board of Higher Education in New York City, are of interest. "I am mindful of the arguments *pro* and *con* as to the wisdom of faculty representation on the board. But one thing seems clear to me: it is less than accurate to assume that the president can and will voice *faculty* sentiment in board deliberations. He can no doubt report it if some effort has been made to find out what it is. Hence I hazard the prophecy that within ten to fifteen years it will become a far more usual practice than now to have direct faculty representation on trustee bodies. . . . I do not say that such a measure will of itself break down the barrier or gulf which so often exists between trustees and faculty; but it should be a gesture of some benefit in that direction." The prophecy, made in 1950, is not being fulfilled. If anything, the distance between faculties and boards, except as bridged by the president, has increased.

In this exclusive working relationship between the president of the college and the board of trustees is to be found one of the most subtle ways by which the board exerts influence over the institution. This influence comes from the simple fact that the president holds office "at the pleasure of the board." So long as he wants to hold the job, he must see to it that it is the board's "pleasure" that he do so. He may risk the displeasure of the faculty, the students, or even the public, so long as he has the board back of him; and, in turn, popularity with the faculty, the students, or the public will not save him if the board is not back of him. An analysis of recent stormy cases in academic history illustrates the principle.

In the famous oath fight in California, President Sproul, believing that he was reflecting the sentiments of the faculty, recommended that the board adopt a loyalty oath for the university. Finding that he was mistaken as to the faculty attitude, he reversed his position and urged the board of trustees to do likewise, much to the latter's displeasure. While the issue was not pressed to a showdown between President Sproul and the board, there is no doubt that the friction with the board was the most serious threat to his position and authority which President Sproul had ever suffered. Conversely, during the stormy years of President Hutchins' reorganization of the University of Chicago, no amount of public or institutional uproar disturbed his command of the situation because of the almost unruffled support he obtained from the board of trustees. On the other hand, at the University of Illinois, President Stoddard resigned immediately, despite widespread support from the faculty, students, and the public, when the board of trustees, although by a narrow margin, adopted a no-confidence vote in his administration. While these situations attracted national interest and attention, countless others, although never reaching the stage of wide public knowledge, illustrate the same principles of the relationship between boards and presidents.

In times of conflict it is tempting to any president to write his insurance, so to speak, with the board. It is by all odds the best unemployment compensation insurance available to him!

Members of boards of trustees differ widely in their interests, their industry, their preparation for their work, and the ways in which, as a board, they wish to operate. Some boards meet frequently and insist upon detailed information; some are content to review general administrative action in the light of broad policies. As practical men, however, the members of boards usually take a greater interest in the housekeeping problems of the institution than they do in matters of educational policy. Buildings and finance are always major interests of trustees—their experience and training make this inevitable as well as most valuable. America's park-like college campuses are monuments to their interest. The planning of a campus can sometimes become the obsession of a board committee or even of a single member, and educational ends may get totally lost somewhere in the planning. The preservation of a quadrangle, or of a memorial tree; the maintenance of a dominant pattern of architecture, or the departure from it; the decision as to whether the next building shall be for science or for the library; these are questions a board is likely to believe it can decide without much help. Trustees, whether as a board or as individual members, more easily see a record in the tangibles of buildings and facilities than in the intangibles of education. This fact is likely to determine the foci of their interests. I have known trustees who followed campus developments with almost the fervor of a superintendent of property.

Finance is the other major area where the practical bent of trustees finds vigorous expression. The experience of business with property and money is, of course, immensely valuable to colleges; but there are, nevertheless, some important differences between educational and business points of view in the management of money and property. For example, trustees nearly always take a conservative "trustee" view of the managemnt of funds. Their first concern is likely to be the conservation or growth of capital. The interest of a college administration which is worthy of its salt is to get income to spend. This is not to say that trustees are not interested in income nor that college presidents are indifferent to preserving capital; but it does mean that there is a basic conflict of interest between the two views as to the management of finance. Trustees are inclined to believe that a college is in good shape if its funds are safe; educators know that you have bought no education until you have spent the money. Colleges are devices for spending, not saving; but it is hard to convince people to whom money is power that money itself is educationally sterile. Endowment funds in I.B.M. stock yielding one per cent may be looking toward the future but the policy ignores the educational needs of the present. Investment is more than conservation and, educationally speaking, the present is always worth more than the future, because the future will be, educationally, the result of the present. The following quotation, in spite of some quaintness of language, breathes a spirit of trustee responsibility which lurks in the members of many boards. One must admire its solid, even if somewhat bleak, conception of duty.

It is the earnest desire of the friends of this institution that it be established and built up by wisdom and stand forever and go on improving like the older institutions of Europe and America. To accomplish this purpose, it is suggested that the Board of Trustees look most critically into the way things are going and make wise provision for future contingencies; if any trustee neglects such care and caution, request him to resign and appoint another. It is a positive wrong to be indulgent to incapacity or inefficiency, to idleness, wastefulness, or any other unfitness. Let them stop all leaks, stir up the indolent, get honest work done and make purchases as far as practicable when prices are lowest, for "there is a time to get." In summer, prepare and lay up for winter. Let them secure every trust, promptly discharge every trustee, officer, agent or employee, and have the business, work, and instruction done by as few men and at as small cost as possible consistent with the true interests of the institution without favor of partiality, remembering that the Lord's work must be done better than our own.[6]

Trustees are also likely to view an unbalanced budget with horror. In part this arises from the habits of business which must show a profit or loss or pay its taxes according to a fixed calendar. Educational institutions are different; they never expect to show a profit; losses are temporary imbalances; they never expect to go out of business. Colleges could profit from far more daring in the management of their finances, in borrowing to provide better facilities, to provide working capital for enterprises which would enable them legitimately to enlarge their income, and to put their own sources of financial support under greater pressure.

Perhaps the most difficult relationship between a college president and a board of trustees lies in the selection, retention, and rewarding of the faculty and staff. Here, in the appointment and review of staff, the board comes nearer to matters of educational policy than in any other of its operations. By its approval or disapproval the board can unmistakably make known its views. Ordinarily boards of trustees, especially of larger colleges and universities, leave the selection of faculty members largely to the administration and content themselves with the reports from the president as to the candidate's qualifications. The interest of a board in the appointment of deans and higher administrators is, of course, more evident and a president will usually clear his recommendations in formal or informal discussion with board members in advance.

Nevertheless, boards are frequently restive about their casual approval of long lists of new appointees, knowing full well that their worst, even if infrequent, difficulties will arise from these

[6] From the charter of Park College, as written by Col. George S. Park, 1875.

very appointments. Furthermore, no board of strong membership likes to be a rubber stamp, approving blindly the important recommendations of administrative officers, no matter how high the board's confidence in the administration may be. No relationship between a president and trustees is more fraught with uneasiness and difficulty than this matter of appointments. A president must be free to negotiate with prospective faculty members and employees; yet no commitment by the president can legally be final until approved by the board. Frequently such board approval cannot be made to fit into a schedule of negotiations. A prospective appointee may have to decide at once which of two offers he will accept, or a vacancy in the faculty may arise unexpectedly; furthermore, if a candidate accepts a president's invitation to join the faculty of an institution, he must be able to rely upon the invitation and to make his plans accordingly. Normally there is no difficulty where the board has delegated the appointment authority or is willing to approve unquestioningly the recommendation of the president. Occasionally, however, a board member will recognize a name in a list which has been placed before them for approval. "Didn't this man run for the legislature once?" or "Didn't I hear that he has advocated the use of oleomargarine instead of butter?" or "Didn't he take part in a radio debate in which he opposed military training?" Questions having been raised, members of a board think that perhaps it would be better to postpone approval until the matter can be looked into a little further. "Of course, there is probably nothing wrong, but delay is the better part of wisdom." The result can be catastrophic not only to the man whose appointment has been recommended for he may already have relinquished his former position, but also to the president who must from now on be uneasy lest *any* commitment of his encounter these unexpected delays or rejections. Furthermore, the college can seldom find a ready substitute for the appointee. Consequently, educational plans are also disrupted.

This event does not need to happen often to cast a shadow of uncertainty over any appointment that is other than routine. An important but subtle consequence of such board action is to make administrators reluctant to negotiate with or to recommend persons prominent enough or sufficiently controversial to provoke board questions. It is better not to recommend than to be embarrassed by rebuff. This problem of the respective authority of presidents as administrators and of boards of trustees as the persons ultimately responsible for the welfare of the institution is a delicate and unresolved aspect of management in higher education.[7]

This illustration of how a board may act on personnel appointments shows how subtly and pervasively it may exercise its influence on all phases of college administration. By its actions the board sets in motion the Law of Administrative Anticipation. This is a universal law wherever authority is exercised. The principle is this: one does not ask for what one knows will be denied or for what may be granted only with reluctance; and one proposes only that which is most likely to be approved.

A college president, familiar with the views of his board, naturally becomes reluctant to risk their impatience and his own embarrassment by asking approval for things which he knows

[7] In an effort to resolve problems of staff appointments, the Board of Trustees of the University of Chicago gave to the chancellor a final right to make even permanent appointments, provided that the departments were consulted and approved the recommendation; or, if public criticism could be anticipated, the case should be referred to the Board before final action. While this potentially narrows the area of difficulty, it does not altogether eliminate it, nor is it likely that many other universities, either public or private, will relinquish with finality such an area of authority and control as the University of Chicago board has done. No doubt the trustees of many of our universities seldom question recommendations for faculty appointments, but the fact that it is always possible affects without question the thought of administrators in formulating their recommendations.

they do not want to approve, or by defending things he knows they do not want defended. If a proposal is likely to raise an issue which he can avoid, it is only natural that he should try to avoid it. As a result he may soon find himself administering the college in its daily operations by saying to his colleagues, "I'm sure the Board would not approve that"; or, "The Board would probably want us to do thus-and-so." In practice, a board comes to mould an institution almost as much by what a president may *expect* it will do as by what it actually does.

But if a board affects the president, the president can also affect the board; indeed, he will be something less than an effective president if he does not. He has several advantages in his favor. He will ordinarily have more information than the trustees; he can shape the agenda of board meetings and thus direct the thought and attention of the board; he is more at home in thinking about education and can state his views and convictions more effectively than can most of the trustees; he can employ delaying tactics until the more disturbing impulses of the board have had time to cool and he has a chance to bring to bear the infinite complexity of education upon that trustee who begins his work by knowing it all. The secret is patience and the skill to let the enterprise itself educate the board.

Laird Bell, the long-time president of the Board of the University of Chicago, has offered college presidents some invaluable advice.

Keep your trustees as fully informed as you can without burying them in reading matter. Tell them the bad news as well as the good—I have found administration prone to tell us how good we are but to forget how good the competition is. Work your trustees and work them hard. Have them meet as often as possible. Put them on committees. Ask them to do special jobs. It is human nature to think most of the things one has worked on. Such activities also teach trustees what colleges and universities are for. It may even make them want to give you some money. It certainly makes them feel what we all want them to feel, that they are truly part of the great adventure of higher education.[8]

Perhaps the most serious of all difficulties faced by boards of trustees arise when they cease to act as a unit and break up into groups or individuals, each guided by particular interests of his own. This is always a threat, but it is likely to become a fact unless a board understands the necessity for unity (not unanimity) and resolutely agrees to oppose such a tendency. Since trustees are usually strong-minded people with varying backgrounds, appointed or elected with different purposes and considerations in mind, who possess differing convictions and interests and varying talents and force of personality, it is no wonder that members tend to ride off in all directions. One member of the board may be intent on seeing that the university establishes a branch in his home community. Another may be interested only in the athletic program. A third may believe that the college glee club should be sent on tour as an instrument of public relations. A fourth has visited the college cafeteria and believes that the students are not being served enough food. A new appointee on the board believes that the president has been in office too long and makes it his immediate mission in life to force his resignation.

The problem of bringing a board together, of inducing it to accept leadership, of developing out of its diversity a united loyalty to themselves as a board and to the institution, is not an easy job. All members of boards are likely to consider themselves born free and equal; it is difficult for them to understand why they should subordinate views they personally hold to views which even a majority of their colleagues hold. It is on this point that all college presidents fervently wish that every trustee would

[8] Laird Bell, "From the Trustee's Corner," *Association of American Colleges Bulletin*, October 1956, pp. 353-361.

take to heart the advice of Charles A. Coolidge, a member of the Harvard Corporation:

> Don't meddle. Don't act as an expert in education. If you hold some pet ideas on education, keep quiet about them. As a layman you should recognize that it is the president's and faculty's job to educate. As a trustee, you should see that these men are capable, and you should not try to do their jobs for them. In short, you should see that the university is well run by someone else, and not try to run it yourself.[9]

---

[9] "Training for Trustees," *Association of American Colleges Bulletin*, December 1956, p. 513.

VI

The President and Public Relations

Public relations, the kind spelled with capitals, has become a force in American life as potent as it is pervasive. At its best it is an elevating influence; informing, educating, persuading. At its worst, it is a technique merely for getting attention, for concealing and disguising, or for making the worse appear the better cause. The art of public relations is in itself neutral, and its devices are equally at the disposal of the worthy and the unworthy. Judgments about the value of public relations are essentially judgments about the causes served and the effects produced.

Public relations has cast its radiant influence over all American education. The results are both good and bad. Public interest in education is higher; its financial support is greater than ever. But it may also be asked whether that very popularity and prosperity have not to some extent been bought at the expense of intellectual and moral independence and vigor.

Every enterprise these days which involves a substantial number of people is affected with a public interest. In this sense there are no private colleges. The public cares less as to whether colleges are classified as public or private than it does about who attends them, who teaches in them, what is taught, and the endless flow of news about their activities. This means public relations, and since every responsibility for the success of the college eventually comes to rest upon the president, he finds himself inextricably a public relations officer. This is true whether it is a large university or a small college, whether public relations are in the main the president's personal responsibility or are shared with a professional staff. In each case the purpose is the same, namely, to create a favorable climate within which the college can operate more easily. Such a climate is too important to be left to chance; it must be created.

Colleges are complex enterprises and there are many "publics" interested in them. This is why the materials and the techniques of their public relations must range over almost the entire spectrum of the advertiser's art. At one end is the presentation of the sober, serious, and dignified products of the best academic minds —the research, the teaching, the scholarship, and the public service. At the other end are the publicity-getting devices of campus scenes, beauty queens, athletic entertainment, and the titillations of coeducation. In between is a boxful of devices of varying usefulness, including the judicious selections of candidates for honorary degrees and big-name commencement speakers. Where the emphasis between extremes is to fall depends upon the institution, the reputation it is trying to create for itself, and the wisdom and skill of those who are trying to create that reputation.

The public relations of colleges falls largely into two categories —the defensive or protective, and the promotional. The first tries to forestall, or at least quickly to minimize, any attention to the institution which is unfavorable. Colleges and universities are the Caesar's wives of our society; any lapses from dull respectability are always exciting but are to be deplored. The newspapers love the lapses and the chronic critics of higher education joyfully

THE PRESIDENT AND PUBLIC RELATIONS 91

exploit them. There is always good copy in campus drinking, the activities of fraternities and sororities, coeducation, and the endless ingenuity with which young people can complicate their own lives and the lives of others. A student hazing tragedy puts M.I.T. far more prominently into national headlines than two Nobel Prize winners. A student invitation to a strip-tease artist to visit the campus of Louisiana State, the alleged torture of a dog in fraternity initiations at U.C.L.A., a "midwinter beach party" at the University of Minnesota, or a lecture by a professional prostitute to a sociology class at the University of Oklahoma, all create prairie fires of publicity, over in a flash but leaving scorched and smoldering feelings and reputations. A casual public may smile tolerantly at such antics but there is always an uneasy, questioning residue in the minds of thoughtful, as well as uninformed, people as to what must go on at such institutions.

There is, of course, always a great temptation on the part of a college to suppress news which would hurt it—the peccadilloes of a professor, the fire in the girls' dormitory, the strike of the power plant employees—but wise men resist the temptation to suppress. Eventually the news will come out and then the suspicion grows that where a little has been reluctantly revealed, there must be a great deal more that is hidden. Experienced college presidents do not suppress news, but one of their most important tasks is to redirect attention and to counter as quickly as possible any unfavorable impressions.

The more important function of college public relations is not, of course, the negative one of defense, but the positive one of promotion. In the large, this means the creation of the favorable conditions and the climate in which the reputation and the resources of the college can grow. The measures of success are to be found in such things as the numbers and quality of the students who apply for admission, the ease with which men of distinction can be attached to the faculty, the financial support which the college can attract, and the development of the esteem with which activities of the college are viewed by its alumni and by the general public. Such esteem may even be brought to the point of affection, reflecting itself in the references middle-aged men make to themselves, without knowing why, as Dartmouth or Michigan men, or Old Tigers, or College '21.

One of the universal techniques which colleges employ in their public relations is the identification and exploitation of any special point or points of distinction to which they can lay claim. The point of distinction may not even be an educational one but it must be respectable and of interest to the public.

Everyone knows Notre Dame as the home of the Fighting Irish, while the University of Chicago is probably better known because it abolished football—a distinction among major universities—than because of any championships it ever won. The University of Washington and the University of Colorado, among their other assets, advertise their salubrious climate, "Summer School Where Summer's Cool." Liberal arts colleges exalt their broad and basic education, "How to Live, Not Merely How to Make a Living"; universities call attention to their breadth of opportunity and their practical curricula. Colleges exclusively for men or for women find quiet ways of implying their superiority to coeducational institutions, and coeducational institutions reply in kind with pointed references to "well-rounded development." Kenyon, Wabash, and Oberlin emphasize the value of limited enrollments; Columbia, New York University, and California make an attractive asset of their size. A private institution implies that it is free from the "restraints" which plague public colleges and universities, while the public institution never lets anyone forget its devotion to "public service." Whatever the point of distinction, the college must discover and refine it, and then ceaselessly hammer it home to students, faculty, alumni, and public.

How important public relations has become may be measured

by the amount of time and attention it now receives. Almost every institution of any size employs a professional staff. In smaller colleges the task is usually a designated part of the responsibility of some administrative office. Whether identified as "public relations," as "information," or even by some less explicit title, the function is the same. With the enormous increase in the size and costs of higher education in recent years, public relations activities have centered more and more around the necessity for raising money. Professional fund-raising organizations, which more and more colleges are using in their financial drives, are little superior if at all to the organizations which many colleges have developed for themselves in their alumni and "development" offices. The persons who head such offices are now frequently given the status of vice presidents, and their skills and techniques are those of the business professional. The national organization of college public relations officers is a strong and growing one.

This growth of attention to public relations not only has value, it is inevitable. No one should believe for a moment, to choose merely conspicuous examples, that Harvard can be successful in an announced drive for eighty-two million dollars, or that the University of Texas can obtain biennial increases in its appropriation, without the most meticulous and continuous practice of professional public relations. Even aside from financial necessity, the organization and activities of higher education are becoming so involved and their importance so great that vast energy must be expended to explain the facts to a busy public. The necessity for interpretive public relations will grow, rather than diminish.

All of these responsibilities of public relations are at once time consuming anxieties as well as opportunities for the president. As a matter of institutional concern as well as self-interest, he gets into the habit of quickly scanning his mail to see what untoward incident or piece of intelligence has outraged some parent or prominent alumnus. He glances through the local paper, braced for some adverse mention of a faculty member, a student party, a misquotation from some of his own remarks, or a leak about college plans. When his phone rings at home he draws a sigh of relief when he finds the message is only another invitation to speak, not a report of a student's suicide, or a report that the springtime epidemic of panty raids has at last reached his own dormitories. The president knows all too well that any breach in the walls of the citadel of respectability over which he presides can require months to repair. If the public or a faculty wants to know what so often breeds in a college president a passion for low visibility, they will find it in the additional anxieties he acquires from high visibility. Presidents know there will be storms enough; is it any wonder they shudder when the boat is needlessly and carelessly rocked?

While public relations is a care to a president, it is also his greatest opportunity. He carries a heavy responsibility for explaining not only his own institution but also the cause of education generally. No one else has so good a rostrum as he; he must use it or betray a trust. No matter how many public relations officers his institution may have, he remains their chief. In fact, it is probably in his public relationships that the college president exerts his greatest influence upon the course of educational development, both within and outside his own institution. His principal device for doing so is to talk; all he needs to do is to accept the invitations to speak which will normally come his way—and then try to have something to say. By no means will all his invitations be opportunities to give the educational word; far too many will be mere occasions of ceremony and duty.

"Duty speeches" are inescapably a large part of a president's obligation, but he can reduce the number of *pro forma* appearances, if he wishes to do so, by letting it be known that he reserves his speeches for serious discussions of education, not for

THE PRESIDENT AND PUBLIC RELATIONS

the crowning of beauty queens or reports to innumerable groups on prospects for next year's halfbacks.

Even so, a conscientious president, eager to win favorable regard for his institution wherever he can, is likely to fall a prey to the pressures of attending an endless number of meetings and responding to the request to "say a few words." Alas! To carry such a burden he must learn a technique of personal survival. He cannot possibly think out something fresh and significant for each occasion (many of them don't deserve it). He learns, like a druggist, to compound his speeches from the fragments he has stored in the vials of his memory.

The art is to say something which, upon evaporation, leaves a favorable impression and no lasting residue of offense or disquieting thought. A possible prescription for such a speech is as follows: One Bright Remark, perhaps his joke for the season, to get attention; a Literary Allusion as a compliment to his audience's education; a Self-Deprecatory Remark, proving that he and his audience are all alike; and finally an Expression of Appreciation for All. The result may be disappointing as an intellectual product; the surprise is that it is no worse. Mass demand can hardly expect the custom-made. With noticeable exceptions, the remarks of American college presidents are frequently bright and clever. They are rarely profound.

From a huge number of factors in the equation of college public relations two can be picked out for closer examination as illustrating most of its complexities. The first of these is the alumni; the second is athletics. These deserve special treatment not only because they involve almost every problem which the colleges encounter and every technique which they employ, but also because they loom large in the lives of most colleges and universities and in the public's acquaintance with higher education.

Everyone remembers the joke about the college president who said that in some future reincarnation he would prefer to be warden of a penitentiary, because he was sure he would not then be troubled with an alumni association. The attachment of an alumnus to his school is essentially a sentimental, not an intellectual, one. The cultivation of this attachment begins as soon as the student registers (sometimes earlier), and its first form is in "school spirit." It thrives on the cultivation of campus traditions and in the development of a warm sense of belonging.[1] The basis thus formed is taken over at graduation by a much more professional and competent alumni organization, whose business it is to prolong this early sentiment into a lifetime of loyalty and to harden it into a sense of duty for the care and support of Alma Mater.

While the characteristics of individual alumni vary greatly, penetrating observers (perhaps with tongues in cheek) have detected three stages in the alumni life-cycle. The first is the sentimental one, which reaches its greatest development about the time of graduation, and may be prolonged for shorter or longer periods thereafter. Some alumni never get over the sentimental stage, and the more superficial professional alumni organizations try to do everything possible to prolong it. The second stage is the "absent-minded" period, in which life closes in, so to speak, on the alumnus. He is busy. If he thinks back to his own education at all, it may be with distaste and irritation as he discovers its shortcomings and inadequacies. He may even feel impatience toward the institution which gave it to him. Its appeals for funds promptly go into the wastebasket; no matter how urgent Alma Mater's needs for money may be, they are less urgent than his own—payments

[1] A great many institutions count as alumni any student who was ever registered, not merely those who have taken degrees; thus, the student who flunked out may find himself welcomed as an alumnus by an institution which would not have him as a student! This leads to varying degrees of alumni warmth and loyalty. An alumnus of Ohio State once remarked with a grin, "The only people I ever meet on Alumni Day are six-weeks Ags," i.e., those who had attended the university for the short courses in agriculture.

on the house, Junior's teeth, the car, the illness of his wife's parents. This absent-minded stage is the longest period in the alumnus life-cycle—the despair of alumni secretaries.

The third may be called the mature stage. By this time the alumnus is considerably older, a little wiser, more secure financially, and more appreciative of the importance of institutions to himself and to society. This stage comes on more rapidly if he has children of his own to educate for parents generally find themselves far more interested in their children's education than they ever were in their own!

Nevertheless, as a mature alumnus, he is less susceptible to appeals to sentiment, more penetrating in his questions, and more critical of the answers. As his interest in education grows he may, however, be less interested in a particular institution, including his own Alma Mater, and more interested in institutions generally which he thinks are "doing a good job." Let it be said to the credit of many a college and university that they have now come to incorporate in their alumni programs elements which are more nearly worthy of the mature alumnus.

Just how much is an active alumni organization worth to a college or to a university? It is a nice question, and there will be outrage and horror in some quarters at the suggestion that it is worth much less than is usually thought. The value, of course, varies widely as between types of schools, the uses made of alumni, and the aggressiveness of alumni interest. Except for a few colleges, Dartmouth, Princeton, Stanford, for example (and even these must be assiduously, even grimly, cultivated), alumni organizations are almost all low-efficiency operations. In proportion to the amount of institutional energy they require for their nurture, their net value is not high, *although it may be crucial.* Indeed, many an institution subsidizes its alumni activities because it believes that it receives from them values of public relations other than financial which make such expenditures worthwhile.

98   THE AMERICAN COLLEGE PRESIDENT

The cultivation of an active alumni interest may even spring occasionally from negative considerations. To put it harshly, the support and good will of the alumni may not in itself mean much to an institution, but its absence can hurt. If there is not an apparent, active, or even noisy alumni support for a school, that fact will have to be explained to legislators, donors, parents, and even prospective students. If there is no enthusiasm from the alumni, why should there be from anyone else? The college which does not spontaneously generate enthusiastic alumni will find it necessary to cultivate them.

In general, women's schools receive less from their alumnae than do men's colleges, and private schools receive more than do state-supported institutions. Some universities and colleges could not balance their budgets except for gifts from the alumni, and where this is the case the institutional anxieties about alumni interest rise proportionately. "Every time I think of trying to get the alumni out of my hair," said the president of one prominent Eastern college, "I ask myself, where else can I get $400,000 a year? I'd rather worry with alumni than try to raise ten million more endowment."

For all their interest, generosity, and indispensability, alumni are for most colleges and universities something of a problem. One difficulty is that of finding anything for them to do. The alumni can be of service to a college in terms of financial support, but aside from that? Even as trustees, alumni have their disabilities. While presumably their interest in their Alma Mater is higher than that of other public-spirited citizens, this interest is frequently offset by their confident knowledge that they alone know how to operate or remake the place, or how to prevent anyone else from doing so. Some institutions use alumni to interview and make reports about prospective students, but this, too, has its doubtful side; the alumnus may be interested in getting Joe or Mary accepted, or may decide quite on his own that the prospec-

THE PRESIDENT AND PUBLIC RELATIONS

tive student isn't "quite the type" no matter how good the brains, and make an adverse report. Aside from a few ceremonial occasions, such as supplying alumni help in organizing meetings when the president or the alumni secretary makes his annual tour, most colleges are at their wits' end to find something, aside from financial support, which can worthily occupy the time and energy of intelligent alumni.

The cultivation of the alumni has its price and it is the president who pays it more than anyone else. The alumni will occupy a major portion of his correspondence. Every alumni gathering wants him as a speaker, and at every gathering he will face alumni in all stages of their life-cycles. He must find a formula to please them all. He must inform without offending, and inspire attachment without making fatal commitments. It is a task for the artist, the diplomat, and the well-conditioned athlete.

Most college alumni are, in their turn, a little bewildered by their own relationship to the college. Since they are ceaselessly asked to maintain their interest in Alma Mater, it is not unnatural that they should expect Alma Mater to maintain an interest in them. If, as they are told, it is "their" school, why shouldn't they assume that they have a right to say something about how it should be run? Many alumni are hurt and puzzled as to why a son or daughter is denied admission. Why shouldn't their support get a student admitted, or entitle them to preferred tickets at football games (it usually does), or get a friend appointed to the faculty, or have a "dangerous" teacher fired, or get someone an honorary degree? Alumni, too, have strong ideas about campus planning; what building to build and where. They do not see why they should not trade their views as the price of their support. The naming of a new building can touch off a major feud; I know of one college which kept money for a new building for fifteen years, while building costs doubled, because no one could break the stalemate as to its location. As one college president said, "I try never to have a tree cut on the campus, no matter how dangerous it has become, until after Alumni Day each spring, and then I have every vestige removed before they get here again. Sometimes," he added sadly, "I get away with it." Progress is suspect to an alumnus if it invokes very much change or destruction. It is a strange relationship between Alma Mater and her grown children.

While there is much that is still childish and immature about alumni activities, and for which the colleges themselves must accept much responsibility, the situation is improving. Colleges today are approaching their alumni, as they are the public generally, with more confident conviction of their own importance and of their rightful claims to mature treatment and generous support. Many alumni prefer to think of themselves as *currently* related to an institution doing something important for students, community, or country than merely to be reminded of a youthful association, some memories of which they might prefer to fade.

It is in the development of this sense of mutual responsibility that the promise of more useful alumni activity exists. It is not the interest of the alumni in the college as such, nor the interest of the college in the individual alumnus which matters so much as it is the common interest of both in the educational work to be done. An alumni association, for example, whose members establish a standing Committee for the Protection of Freedom of Speech for Professors at the college, or who adopt resolutions calling for higher admission requirements for freshmen, or set up a fund for the college authorities to use where they think it is most needed, will not only have become allies in the Great Cause, they will find for themselves as alumni a much greater sense of satisfaction.

Another element of the public relations complex with which American higher education finds it difficult to come to terms is athletics. Conditioned to associate athletics with education all through the grades and high schools, the public naturally accepts athletics as a part of college education as well. At the college level, however, athletics undergoes a transformation. In a great many institutions it ceases to be student recreation, which is normally and naturally a part of student life, and becomes public entertainment, an activity which has little to do with education. This transformation takes place whenever specialized coaches are selected, and when players are chosen in order to win games rather than to play them.

It is this shift of emphasis which draws a line between the student and the athlete. The interest of the college in the student lies in what it can do for him; its interest in the athlete lies in what he can do for it. The recruited athlete has no value to the college unless he can play well—well enough, in fact, to attract the interest of the public to the games. Since the public is interested in athletics, the cultivation of athletics by the college, beyond the legitimate point of student recreation, is an attempt to capitalize on this public interest and to divert it to the college itself. In short, although colleges are educational institutions, their highly organized athletic programs are public entertainment.

Any college in America which lives with intercollegiate athletics will have its troubles; if it tries to live without intercollegiate athletics, it will have a different set of troubles. This is why athletics, as a public relations problem, is infinitely complex and difficult. The problems are merely different, when the program is low-key, as at Amherst, Williams, or Western Reserve, from those which arise when athletics is an indispensable part of successful institutional operation, as at Notre Dame, Michigan, or U.C.L.A. Reed College, the University of Chicago, New York University, which try to get along without football, have their problems in attracting undergraduates because, it is assumed, there must be "something queer" about such schools. The alumni grumble and the trustees wonder whether the students who do come are the same as the red-blooded variety who go elsewhere.

While the big-time athletic programs of other institutions solve *these* problems, they create others for themselves. As Minnesota's President Morrill said, "Next to a losing football team, a winning one is a disaster." A university which doesn't occasionally win a championship is in for difficulty. When it engages in big-time athletics it is clear that it has paid the price for success; but without the prize of success it will eventually be convicted of bad management. Schools which on occasion drastically de-emphasize, such as Pittsburgh, Fordham, Tulane, or Northwestern, find life miserable unless they reform; and schools not quite "in the swim," such as Western Reserve or Johns Hopkins, wonder continually whether they would be better off if they were.

Every president of an athletics-minded college knows that he stands on an active volcano. Reconciling the recruitment of competent athletes with conventional scholarship programs is an impossibility; yet it is equally embarrassing for a president to admit frankly that his college is in the business of entertaining the public, and that in order to be successful it is necessary to secure the entertainers. Almost every university president has suffered from this schizophrenia. Sometimes the effort is made by athletic staffs and administrative subordinates to "protect" the president from embarrassing knowledge as to the true state of affairs. While the president may thus have a kind of artificial innocence, he is often placed in the position of having everybody else know what presumably he should know best. If a president isn't interested in being protected (and a number could be named who wanted no such "protection") it may be necessary to protect him anyway, by organizing athletic control outside of the jurisdiction of the president. This method of placing athletic control nominally in the hands of so-called independent student organizations, as at the Universities of California, Washington, North Carolina, and a

THE PRESIDENT AND PUBLIC RELATIONS 103

number of others, has some conveniences for hiding skeletons but it does not relieve the uneasiness of conscientious or sophisticated administrators. Presidents in such institutions who are inclined to become inquisitive about athletics are usually encouraged to find other interests.

Nevertheless, the presidents of most institutions engaged in big-time athletics must be grateful that they know no more than they do. As they address platitudes to the end-of-the-season football banquets and make a few remarks between halves to packed stadiums, they also know that any day they may be made to plead guilty that they did not know what they should have known about the practices of their athletic departments, or, knowing them, did nothing.

It is safe to say that most of the larger colleges and universities in the country operate athletic programs which are governed more nearly by the requirements of public entertainment than by the needs and interests of their students. A president who would seek to treat such an athletic program in purely educational terms will do so at his peril. Athletics represents one of the most difficult moral problems which face American higher education. The president of any college with an athletic program will find himself at some time in need of every art of public relations; he had also better be not too concerned about a course of personal consistency.

The sum of public relations for all college presidents has become an incredibly complex equation whose variables are constantly getting out of balance. The president's mind must be an electronic calculator which can give him instantly some estimate of the effect of any event, proposal, comment, or utterance upon the faculty, students, alumni, legislators, donors, critics, and friends. As a man of courage, his impulse may be to say "Damn the torpedoes" and sail straight ahead. But if he does, he may be sure that he will encounter torpedoes and, more likely than not, he will get sunk. There are explosive forces in American higher education and the president who wishes to survive them will treat them with wariness and respect.

In this age, publicity is a necessity for the successful operation of any public enterprise. In this sense, all colleges are public enterprises and the president must get publicity for his college. To serve a useful purpose, publicity must be favorable; to be favorable, it must not offend. This is where the roles of public relations and of education are often fundamentally in conflict. Education, by its nature, is dedicated to change, to the improvement of the individual and of society. This mission it cannot accomplish without implied, and frequently explicit, criticisms of both the individual and society. The role of public relations is to please as many people as possible. Consequently, the temptation of the college president is to reduce himself and his institution to an innocuous role, to speak ringingly of that which already has public approval, and to avoid reference to that which carries the risk of criticism and unpopularity. Leadership has always required that sometimes the backs of leaders be turned toward those whom they lead.

Fortunately, conflict between public relations and education does not always present itself so starkly, though it is nearly always present in some degree. There are thoughtful people in almost all the publics of a college or a university who will accord it some measure of continuing support, even when critical of particular policies and acts. There is a considerable public which, in spite of all the clutter of press agentry, sensationalism, and artificiality, will render good education the respect it deserves. The college president who does not want to spend his life cultivating popularity can really strive to establish respect for himself and for his college. Respect can itself sometimes be transformed into a kind of popularity, but the two are rarely synonymous.

Nevertheless, there is room for the president to practice a type of public relations appropriate to the legitimate mission of his institution. To limit its public relations to that type alone will tax every capacity of his character and mind. Institutions dedicated to the search for truth must also be dedicated to its practice. They must be truthfully represented, and the president who is clear in the exposition of educational matters, whose convictions are held and expressed with honesty, and who, while criticizing, does not forget to praise, can still find, if he wishes to do so, considerable freedom for his work.

VII

The President Among Scholars

"No COLLEGE or university is better than its faculty." The sentiment is as true as it is trite, and it identifies for a president his most important job—to get and to keep effective the best faculty he can. This is his most difficult task. Clear, studious minds, devoting themselves to the discovery, organization, and presentation of truth in the classroom and in scholarly publications are the heart of education. No matter what the price necessary to keep such minds lively, productive, and devoted to their work, the result is a bargain for our colleges and universities and for our society. Unhappily for college presidents, the difficulty of the task is proportional to its importance.

The effectiveness of a faculty is greatly hindered or enhanced by the "administration"—the faculty name for the organizational apparatus identified with the president.[1] To be effective, the faculty must look to the president to do three things: to state the ends which the college and hence the faculty are trying to serve,

[1] A younger president of one of our larger Eastern colleges, finding the "administration" constantly referred to by the faculty, burst out to a colleague: "If they mean me, why don't they say so!" In time he became accustomed to the euphemism. The semantic device has its usefulness, however, for presidents as well as faculties.

and to set the tone of the enterprise; to provide the means which will enable the faculty to do its work well; to maintain the necessary conditions of academic freedom. Any one of these tasks is sizeable; the three will keep the president incessantly busy.

A college which lacks a clear idea of where it is going or of what it is trying to do will suffer from aimlessness, and so will its faculty and administrators. Whether it is a secular liberal arts college, a church-related school, or a complex university, clarity of purpose is necessary. Without it there can be little in common among those who operate or support it, and little or no guidance by which to select and organize the means appropriate to its purposes. The constant discussion of what their institutions were educating people *for* and hence what means were appropriate to that end is what has distinguished America's most influential college presidents—Wilson, Eliot, Jordan, Butler, Harper, Hutchins, and a half-dozen others.

It is primarily upon the president that the responsibility falls for being clear and articulate about what the college is trying to do. This sense of guiding purpose translates itself into the daily operation of the college by determining what support it will seek and what it must avoid, what kinds of faculty and students it wants and what their preoccupations should be, what kinds of activities it will encourage or discourage, and, when new things are to be undertaken, what these are to be. The president must himself be clear as to what kind of enterprise it is he presides over. He must be able to see what is in keeping with its nature and he must also be able to see that some things are as incompatible with it as, say, smoking would be in church.

Since to the world the president is the spokesman for the college, he becomes inevitably the spokesman, so far as the world is concerned, for the faculty as well. If he states a philosophy which makes the work of the college significant, the faculty who do the work will feel significant. If he inspires pride and conviction, if he embodies in his personality and in his own practice the educational ends he has in view for the college, the faculty will feel that he does for all of them what each might like to do for himself. If he does not, the faculty will feel voiceless, or apologetic.

The second expectation which the faculty makes of the president is that he provide them with the facilities by which to carry on their work effectively. By the word "facilities" the faculty means everything they need—books, space, salaries, equipment, buildings, help, time—together with competent administrative organization and management. It is quite an order, but a reasonable one. It is, so to speak, a part of the contract: the faculty will do the teaching and research, the administration must make it possible for the faculty to do so.

In summary the formula sounds simple; in application it is infinitely complex. The acquisition, distribution, and management of the facilities absorb most of the administrative energies of the college. The choices are endless—they may range from a new electric typewriter for the dean's office or another calorimeter in chemistry to the establishment of a distinguished professorship or the development of a new art center. In the welter of daily operations, the interplay of personalities, the ever-present limitations of resources, the changing pressures from outside or within, unless the greatest care is taken the relations of a president and a faculty can get terribly tangled.

The president must understand from the outset that, while this expectation on the part of the faculty for the things it needs is a proper one, it is one he can never meet. The demands of education are boundless, but it is a part of his contract to supply as many of them as he can. For him there can be no rest. He learns to live with the ceaseless pressure for "more"—more buildings, more books, more money. Since it is his duty to provide these things, he can expect little gratitude or praise for doing his duty but he can be justly blamed if he does not. As President Hutchins bluntly put it, there is no way for him to win and many ways to lose! Nevertheless, this is the nature of the task of the college president, and he has no right to complain when its truth fully dawns upon him.

The most insistent problem which has emerged in the discussions of financing higher education and hence of the president's financial responsibilities is faculty salaries. Improvement in the pay of teachers has not kept pace with that of most other professional and occupational groups. Among teachers themselves the status of college teachers has deteriorated more than that of others.[2] Unless it is corrected such a trend can have only one consequence—a steady decline in the power of the academic career to attract able young people. And such a consequence, long continued, is, for our society, unthinkable. This is why the matter of teachers' salaries is so important to every aspect of the administration of colleges and universities.

Why the problem of teachers' salaries, particularly for college teachers, is so acute is a complex phenomenon. The basic difficulty is that the people of the United States have not yet fully awakened to the increasing indispensability of higher education nor to the consequences, financial and social, of the demand on the part of more people for more education. They have not appreciated the fact that, quite aside from the decline in the value of the dollar, aside from larger enrollments and expanding curricula, *better* education costs more money.

The effects upon faculty members and upon institutions of this failure of the American people are varied and subtle. For example, faculty members as a group have little influence upon the level of their own salaries, for they are not a bargaining unit and, unlike doctors and lawyers, they do not make their own jobs. Unless they go outside the college walls they have scant opportunity to

[2] Beardsley Ruml and Sidney G. Tickton, *Teaching Salaries Then and Now*, Bull. No. 1, The Fund for the Advancement of Education, 1955.

enlarge their incomes. They are dependent upon the financial strength of their institutions. This not only varies widely but also rests far more in the hands of others—president, board, or legislature—than in their own. As they sense the inflationary climate, see the rising incomes in occupations which are less demanding, and share the normal aspirations for better living for themselves, their frustration intensifies their anxieties and restiveness.

All of this has several unhappy consequences. One is to intensify intra-faculty rivalries for tenure, promotions, and a larger share of such salary increments as are possible. Another is to hold the "administration" responsible for the failure to meet faculty needs and expectations. This, in turn, drives presidents to desperate measures to meet faculty expectations with the result that dependent and frustrated faculties and harried presidents begin to look upon each other as irritating causes of their respective troubles.

Nevertheless, faculty members do take steps, not as a group but as intelligent individuals, to ease their financial stringency. Some leave the profession. A large number of others, particularly in the universities, are turning more and more to outside sources to supplement their incomes—contract research, consultant services of every kind, lecturing, and textbook writing. Vacations, long regarded as periods which the teacher properly devoted to study and reflection for the sake of his profession, have become, of necessity, periods for making money, frequently in completely alien employment. The question of what constitutes "full-time" for faculty employment has become for many institutions a serious and thorny administrative problem. These supplementary incomes from outside sources have now become so common among faculties and so large a factor in their total compensation that the fact must be weighed carefully in estimating their financial status and needs.[3]

[3] H. E. Longnecker, *University Faculty Compensation Policies and Prac-*

If rivalry among faculty members is intensified by financial stringency, so is rivalry among institutions. Where money becomes such a crucial factor of competition, smaller or poorer colleges are constantly being raided by larger or richer schools and are compelled to recruit less well-qualified teachers. Moreover, in their desire to hold or to attract particular individuals, institutions often make arrangements which create wide disparities in salaries, adding further to the problems of faculty morale for themselves and rival schools.

What are the long-range effects of these influences upon the teaching profession itself? Perhaps the most serious is the infiltration of the money-making spirit and the loss of the single-mindedness which higher education demands of its devotees. The truth is that teaching, especially in urban centers and in our larger colleges and universities, is becoming a part-time occupation, with the attendant educational and professional difficulties that might be expected. As William James long ago pointed out, teaching is a tyrannical profession, never allowing enough hours in the day nor years in a lifetime to do all that it demands. To divert, either from choice or necessity, time and energy already insufficient for the profession's needs is to enervate it still further. This is what is happening in our colleges and universities.

Yet the academic world cannot blame all of its financial troubles upon a lag in the public's appreciation for its services. If it did not originate the difficulties of which it rightfully complains it has, at least, compounded them. Enrollments have grown and tuition has risen, with large corresponding increases in college and university income. There have been greatly enlarged gifts, endowments, and public appropriations, yet the salary of the college professor has not shared proportionately in these economic improvements. Why? At least a part of the answer lies in the failure of the col-

---

tices in the U. S., a report to the Association of American Universities, 1956.

leges—faculty and administrators—to get themselves under control. While the gross incomes of the colleges and universities have been doubling and trebling, so have the numbers of their courses, even though students can take only the same number of units for graduation and spend the same number of years in study. At the same time, the number of courses taught by faculty members has, on the average, declined; the decline being most drastic in the universities rather than in the colleges. The ratio of teachers to students is now about one to ten, which should be a sufficiently obvious explanation as to why the incomes of colleges must be spread so thinly in the pay envelopes of the professors.

What will improvement require? Some improvement will have to be found in larger amounts of public and private support. But it will require more.

A reorganization of the curriculum, facilities and teaching aids at all levels of the educational process is overdue and inevitable—both to reverse the trend to economic deterioration and to meet the requirements of increased enrollments. The situation will be met not with more money only, but with increased efficiency, new ideas on teaching methods, drastic reorganization of the curriculum. . . .[4]

In short, the financial plight of higher education must be cured not only by those who support it, but also by those who are in it.

In addition to their expectation of the president as spokesman and as provider, faculties have one other major expectation, that he maintain conditions of academic freedom. This is the expectation to which faculties are probably more sensitive than to any other.

No long exposition of the nature of academic freedom is in order here, but enough needs to be said to indicate the complexities of the subject for both presidents and faculties.[5] Academic

---

[4] Ruml and Tickton, *op. cit.*, p. 25.

[5] An excellent review of the subject of academic freedom will be found in R. Hofstadter and W. P. Metzger, *The Development of Academic Free-*

freedom may be defined theoretically as the right of the teacher to pursue the truth. Practically, it is more accurate to describe it as the scope the teacher has to study, teach, and say what he pleases so long as he remains within the limits allowed by the particular institution and the society within which he works.

While academic freedom never exists without some limits the important thing to remember is that the *work* of a college or university cannot be done without a substantial degree of such freedom. The search for truth involves investigation, criticism, doubt, and competition. If these things cannot exist or be carried on freely the search itself is discouraged or destroyed. Without academic freedom, academic institutions become instruments of propaganda. The academic world is united in its belief that freedom is essential for its work. Debates on the subject are less frequently about academic freedom in the abstract than they are about it in the concrete.

Cases of serious conflict over academic freedom are almost never simple. This is why presidents may often seem slow to mount the battlements. It is not that they are necessarily craven and timid men; rather, they know that institutions do not flourish well in an atmosphere of conflict, and if conflict can be avoided this seems to them one form of good. Hence the first reaction of a president may be one of annoyance toward a faculty member who has created or raised an issue of academic freedom. Sometimes presidents in their efforts to avoid conflict and placate complaining groups have gone so far as to apologize for the offending faculty members, while at the same time trying to avoid any administrative action by carefully explaining that tenure regulations prevent them from invoking penalties they imply they would otherwise bring to bear. Any such avoidance of the issue is,

---

dom in the United States (New York: Columbia University Press, 1955). This book is a rich historical and philosophical interpretation of higher education in the United States.

of course, inexcusable, and a faculty quickly and justifiably resents such double talk.

College presidents know as well as faculties do that education is not implicitly devoted to the maintenance of the *status quo;* but they also know the consequences to all concerned if the conflict with the *status quo* is too much in evidence. Presidents know that issues of academic freedom once joined can often have nothing but unfortunate results. Recent "security" cases involving the membership of faculty members in the Communist Party are cases in point. Former President Wriston of Brown University has made a summary statement worth pondering:

> Among all the instances wherein I have seen the tenure of a teacher impaired or destroyed on an issue which involved freedom of opinion within his field of teaching and research I have never known one where the merits were all on one side. Usually the man was asking for trouble. Usually, on the other hand, the institutional representatives handled the issued ineptly or unfairly—and in every instance the gains resulting from his displacement were more than offset by the losses.[6]

Many a faculty member does not realize how frequently he is defended without ever having known that he was under attack. The mail that comes to the president about Professor Jones' speech before the Rotary, or about what was said in the course on comparative religion about religious cults, or the discussion of sex variants in abnormal psychology, must be handled tactfully. If the complaint is relayed to the professor it may cause fear, anger, or an unhealthy self-consciousness in class. Here is where a president and the faculty can be grateful for help from a wise and experienced dean or department head.

It is thus clear that a college president assumes for a faculty a heavy—if not impossible—burden of expectation. This he can bear

---

[6] Henry M. Wriston, "Academic Tenure," *The American Scholar*, 1939–40, vol. 9, pp. 341–342.

more cheerfully, however, if he has thought deeply about the teaching profession and about the feelings, problems, characteristics, and even the eccentricities of faculty members. If he understands some of their strains he can bear his own more easily.

The president must understand, among other things, the peculiar value of job security to faculty members, not only as an adjunct of academic freedom but also as a necessary freedom from personal anxiety in order that they may concentrate more effectively upon teaching and scholarship. The president should also understand the hazard of boredom in teaching—perhaps its greatest hazard. Each year the professor faces a new group of students remarkably like those of last year in age, appearance, and preparation. He attempts to teach them about the same thing with about the same results. (The teacher who is scandalized at the suggestion of boredom in teaching and who asserts brightly that his feeling of kinship with students has remained over the years exactly what it always was, probably suffers a little from arrested development himself!)

A more trying trait which can develop as an occupational hazard for the college professor is arrogance. This grows out of the easy victories of the classroom where he works with young people who know less than he does. He may thus unconsciously come to believe that business, politics, and educational administration would be much better managed if those in charge would only apply the same intelligence to their work that he uses in his own. The capacity of the college professor to be critical of the world around him is in part the luxury of a man whose own world is more nearly subject to his own control.

One other thing the college president keeps in mind if he wishes to understand the faculty. This is the tyrannical nature of the teaching profession, its haunting sense of things undone. During every waking hour the conscientious college professor feels driven by his inadequate preparation for teaching, by the books he has not yet read, the articles not yet written, the ideas not yet clearly formulated. Inside or outside the classroom and laboratory he carries this guilty load, and it creates for him a sense of strain and indeed a continuity of labor not adequately reflected in the formal teaching schedule. This is why the professor so often feels overworked; he may have a sense of working terribly hard when no one else can see that he is doing anything. Indeed, he *may* be working hard when no one else can see that he is working at all. It is also possible for him to mislead himself into believing he is working hard when in fact he is only dreading it.[7]

The president must try to understand the problems and the psychology of the faculty members; he must make administrative accommodations for them. He can help the faculty combat boredom, insecurity, arrogance, overwork, and other occupational hazards by provisions for tenure regulations, sabbatical leaves, varied committee assignments, and other devices which opportunity or ingenuity will suggest. Above all, he must not fret or grow impatient with what seem on occasion vague and captious faculty complaints. An exchange of letters between Dean Francis P. Keppel of Columbia College and President Butler illustrates the point. Wrote Keppel:

There is a certain undercurrent of dissatisfaction about the place, and . . . I make bold to suggest that when you get back in your office you get say a half dozen of the good men who are "upsot," and let them get their troubles off their minds.

To which President Butler replied:

If you will tell me specifically who the dissatisfied people are, and what they are dissatisfied about I shall be glad to see what I can do to make them happier. I cannot, however, undertake to turn my office

[7] I have suggested that the engineering faculty should invent for the teaching profession a "strain gauge" which could measure for each professor his feeling of effort in connection with his work! Administrators find that the efforts to equate or even to measure teaching loads in terms of hours or of student loads are not very satisfactory.

into a sanatorium for academic hypochondriacs. *Le malade imaginaire* belongs to the job of the Professor of dramatic literature. The fact of the matter is that a good many men who are in the academic career make a mistake of choosing it; and when they find this out it is often too late for them to change and there is nothing left for them but everlasting fretfulness and fault finding. About all that one can do for them is to provide as much sweet oil as will suffice for a libation. . . .[8]

It is the president's job to interpret and defend the academic life to those who understand it less well. If, accustomed himself to more definable tasks than those of the faculty, he becomes occasionally impatient with what seem to him their slipshod and leisurely operations, let him remember that *his* kind of schedule and responsibilities can never produce either good scholarship or good teaching.

If the faculty is the best measure of the quality of a college or university it follows that the best way, perhaps the only way, genuinely to improve an institution is through raising the quality of the faculty. For all practical purposes this can be accomplished only at the time of selection by the process of replacing with people who are better qualified those who die, retire, or resign. (Do college teachers really improve or do they just carry out over the years their original promise?)

Consequently, the selection of faculty members is the president's most important job; it is also his hardest. Daniel Coit Gilman, the first president of Johns Hopkins, remarked at the close of his career that he laid aside the task of building a faculty with a sigh of relief. Here are a few of the things that make the task so hard. First, there are not enough first-class, trained brains to man the college classrooms in America; the classrooms are too numerous, good minds too scarce and in too great demand in other

---

[8] *Appreciations of Frederick Paul Keppel* (New York: Columbia University Press, 1951), pp. 13–14.

fields as well. The job of the president is to get as many exceptional minds as he can. Fortunately, even a few on a campus have an energizing effect, far beyond their numerical strength, on both students and faculty colleagues.

Secondly, since all colleges are really looking for the same people, namely, the small number with exceptional minds and training, the competition for them is fierce. The winners, for the most part, are the schools with the most money, the most inviting opportunities for professional success, the highest prestige. To this generalization there are some exceptions: dedicated people who are loyal to a particular institution or type of education, and those occasional, bright individualists who eschew the usual forms of academic success.

Thirdly, the highly specialized training of faculty members today makes their qualifications difficult to assess or compare. Fourthly, faculty members, like everyone else, are subject to change, and the man of great promise at thirty may be, even at forty, merely a man who *had* great promise. "Time and chance happeneth to them all," and a college lives with its choices a long time.

The influence of what I shall call the "big-university" pattern of academic success is one of the most powerful forces in American higher education. It consists of larger salaries than most liberal arts colleges can pay, of lighter teaching loads, of greater opportunity for research and scholarship, for teaching graduate students, and, from the combination of these things, for building reputation. There is no doubt that success in such an academic environment takes brains, training, energy, and a strong competitive instinct. The rewards, to those who possess these capacities, are satisfying and commensurate with the effort. Hence those persons who give promise of fulfilling the big-university pattern of success are constantly seeking, or are being sought by, the institutions which offer it. Graduate students, trained in such institutions,

THE PRESIDENT AMONG SCHOLARS

are indoctrinated in these conceptions of success long before they get their advanced degrees. Thus the image of the successful professor and the successful institution tends to perpetuate itself.

Whatever the drawbacks to such a pattern of academic life it must be said that it offers a wide variety of activity to people of exceptional talent. One of the challenges facing colleges which may not wish to succumb to the pattern is how to find equivalent professional satisfactions for their able faculty members.

In spite of all these hazards, the exercise of care, study, and good judgment in choosing faculty members is worthwhile, no matter what the state of the market, or of the competition. Even so, the president's influence on the selection of faculty, unless the college is small, is more indirect than direct—for the most part he must make choices from those who are recommended to him.[9] It is rare indeed that he can or should take the actual selection of faculty members out of the hands of schools or departments. A few presidents have tried it, and the results have been almost always disastrous—the lesson of history is that court favorites are never popular.

Moreover, looking for faculty members is a time-consuming job, and the president does not have the time. The people "in the field," especially in these days of specialization, will know the names and location of the most likely candidates and they will consider themselves, logically and rightly, as the best judges of the candidate's qualifications, including his acceptability as a colleague.

The president can, however, be a major factor in the selection of faculty members by keeping control of the process by which

[9] Of course this is not true where new faculties are being organized. Gilman at Johns Hopkins, Harper at Chicago, Jordan at Stanford, all had the opportunity of assembling almost singlehandedly the original stars of their faculties. It is true also, of course, that presidents of great personal charm, reputation, or strength of character can attract persons to their institutions who would not otherwise come.

appointments are made. He does, after all, have a power to veto; it may be unwise for him to nominate, but he certainly has a right to object. This is a strategic power. By letting administrators know what kinds of qualifications are acceptable, and by asking the right kinds of questions, the president can profoundly influence the character of the recommendations laid before him. He can ask: who recommends the nominee; who else was considered; what distinguishes this nominee from other candidates; where have they looked, and are there other persons who have not yet been considered? If departments are faced with the necessity of explaining and defending the recommendations they make, the president will have exerted substantial pressure. He should be wary, however, of substituting his own preferences or judgment for the preferences or judgments of those more familiar with a field of knowledge. Aside from other complications he may find that his crystal ball is no better than theirs.

To what extent and in what ways should a faculty share in the administration of a college or university? In practice the answers range from virtually complete faculty control to complete faculty exclusion, from democracy to dictatorship. The great majority of colleges distribute themselves along the spectrum in between. No question is a livelier subject of faculty or presidential discussion.[10]

The case for a large measure of faculty participation in administration is easy to formulate. The arguments are the arguments for democracy itself. The faculty see the college or university not as employer with themselves as employes, but as a community of which they are members. Their teaching and scholarship they see not as products bought or sold, but as a kind of art best produced and most effective when created under conditions

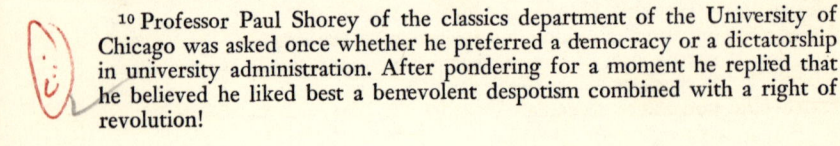

[10] Professor Paul Shorey of the classics department of the University of Chicago was asked once whether he preferred a democracy or a dictatorship in university administration. After pondering for a moment he replied that he believed he liked best a benevolent despotism combined with a right of revolution!

of self-direction. Who should know better than a faculty how best to organize the conditions of learning or of teaching? How can a faculty carry out its responsibilities except by sharing in the creation and management of the means by which the responsibilities can be discharged? These are persuasive arguments, so persuasive in fact that most institutions of higher education accept them and provide in some degree for faculty participation in administration.

There is no doubt that faculties have both knowledge and wisdom, and the good management of a college requires all the knowledge and wisdom which can be brought to bear. Yet faculties have serious shortcomings as administrative bodies. Faculties may still be what we are fond of calling "communities of scholars" (although it requires considerable courtesy now to include all the varied activities of higher education under this term), but they are more; they are aggregations of human beings who are much like everyone else. This means they have their full quota of passions and preferences, ambitions, rivalries, differences of educational interests, experience, and outlook. As the tendency toward specialization grows, their differences become more pronounced. In larger institutions faculty separation leads to a lack of institutional unity; in smaller colleges faculty differences intensify through too intimate acquaintance. When Henry Adams wanted to indicate his contempt for the small-mindedness of congressional debates he said that they were as bad as a Harvard faculty meeting.

Yet it is not the growth of disunity within faculties themselves which handicaps their administrative effectiveness so much as it is the fact that colleges now require so much more administration than formerly. Matters of property, contracts, accounting and finance, union organizations, zoning regulations, liability insurance, social security, and a thousand other items are too far removed from the classroom for the faculty to be well-informed about them, quite aside from the faculty time which would be consumed in their management. Even on matters such as their own tenure, salaries, and conditions of employment generally, faculty administration cannot be unrestricted for the simple reason that men are not good judges in their own cases. Faculties which become deeply involved in the determination of their own status (and there are a number of institutions which illustrate the principle) tend to become obsessed with matters which have a strong personal flavor. It is normal for people to think of their personal comforts and advantages, and where they are free to determine these for themselves they can hardly be blamed for taking advantage of the opportunity.

The meticulousness of the faculty mind as well as its specialized preoccupations is another administrative disability. Faculty members are intelligent and articulate—"he does not believe a thing has really been said until he has said it"—and they are also perfectionists. Hence they tend to require an inordinate amount of time for the disposition of relatively simple matters. If they look for it, some faculty members can almost always find hidden importance in any detail.

Yet, on the other hand, administration cannot be left to administrators. The wisdom, the experience, and the *interests* of the faculty require direct representation. This becomes more difficult as management becomes more complex and more highly organized and as the separation between faculty and administration in their division of labor becomes more pronounced. At one stage in our institutional development it was generally believed that some division of powers might be achieved, a parceling out of academic matters—admission requirements, curricula, degrees—to the faculty, and a reservation of management responsibilities—finance, buildings, personnel—to the president and the administration. But such dividing lines have become steadily less useful and more indistinct. Every "academic" matter seems to involve "administration," and every administrative action seems to affect an academic interest. A faculty might use its authority to vote higher entrance requirements—but at the expense of reducing needed enrollments? The administration might be offered a million dollars for a new school—shall it ask the faculty whether to accept?

A formal division of labor between faculties and administrators in terms of subject matter seems less and less feasible. The pressures of time, specialization of interests, inertia on the one hand, and the necessity for action on the other, are factors which destroy such formulae. Actually, I think the influence of faculties in the administration of colleges and universities generally has declined in the post-war era, both as to the degree of their participation and in their effectiveness. In part, this is due to factors already mentioned—the growth of specialization and resulting faculty disunity, the increase in size and unwieldiness of institutions, the incompatibility of faculty mental habits with administrative detail. Perhaps even more responsible, however, for the decline of faculty influence has been the growth of "outside" factors which make the institutions themselves less self-controlled than they used to be—a general tightening of the society of which they are a part, the suffusing influence of national defense, and the force of public relations appearing in a hundred variations. Always poorly organized and haphazardly led, faculties have not been able to cope with flank attacks from such disparate forces.[11]

What part, then, can faculties play in the administration of colleges and universities? They can play the full part which their

[11] As an illustration, take the post-Sputnik outburst of public discussion of education. Faculties as individuals or as organized groups have had much less to say than have college presidents, publicists, and even government officials. Eventually, all of this discussion of educational reform will have to be translated into curricula reorganization and an improved quality of instruction. Achieving this in the face of faculty inertia or active resistance is an awesome prospect. Organized faculties can subject any educational reform to searching review, but it is extremely difficult for them to initiate such reforms.

time, wisdom, and experience entitle or will permit them. But this part they play through consultation rather than through the exercise of administrative authority—through influence, not power. In matters of college administration faculties should have the privileges which Walter Bagehot attributed to the King of England: "the right to be consulted, the right to encourage and the right to warn." These rights should be *guaranteed* to the faculty by processes which administrators *must* observe, but when the processes have been observed the subsequent responsibility for decision is the responsibility of the administrator. If then he decides unwisely he does so at his peril. For the faculty the subtlety of the formula lies in the fact that it can thus exercise influence without suffering the distractions of power.

Just as the management of higher education has grown to the point where faculties, in order to care adequately for the expanding demands of teaching and scholarship, have had to relinquish a substantial degree of administrative control, so presidents whose primary responsibility is administration have been compelled to watch their influence on the more intimate matters of education steadily decline. By the more intimate matters of education I mean those related to the work of the classroom—what is taught, to whom, and how. Even the general *shape* of education, aside, perhaps, from an occasional expression of concern about "the humanities" or "education for citizenship" or the value of "liberal education," has got beyond presidential control. Among the myriad forces converging upon colleges, from within the campus and without, the president serves as an educational arbiter of competing claims, a broker trying hard to reconcile equitably the various bids for the interest, time, and resources of faculty, students, and institution.

The decline or, perhaps, one should say, the transformation, of the influence of college presidents upon the more purely intellectual life of their institutions is due, as has been said, to the growth

THE PRESIDENT AMONG SCHOLARS

of specialization and a further refinement in the division of labor in higher education. No matter how much each might wish it otherwise, the evolution of the colleges and universities is forcing presidents to be managers and faculties to be scholars. For presidents there is a law of primacy: the more insistent administrative duty drives out the less insistent intellectual interest. Eventually his preoccupation with "housekeeping," however irritating and deplorable it may be to a new president of scholarly interests, weans the mind and creates a mood of resignation. Soon he finds his colleagues making references to books he has not read, discussions he has not heard about. Eventually, he hears them using a new and unfamiliar scholarly jargon. Sadly he is compelled to accept the fact that he really is no longer "up with the field." The phenomenon is universal; the process, longer and more painful for some than for others.[12]

There recently have been and still are (and, let us hope, will continue to be) those valiant presidents who have refused to accept their banishment from the direct educational activities of their schools. Usually they are presidents who, previous to their elevation, had strong convictions as to what should be taught, how it should be taught, and what the intellectual results should be.

[12] In such gatherings of presidents as those of the National Association of State Universities, the Association of American Colleges, and the Association of American Universities, all the moods and stages of presidential development are consciously and unconsciously revealed in the privacy of personal communication. Some presidents with genuine scholarly skills and interests are saddened by their personal deprivation. They speak plaintively of presidential concerns confined to loaves and fishes. Those who no longer suffer from twinges of scholarly nostalgia listen with varying degrees of tolerance or impatience. The presidential state of mind may eventually become a serious matter of faculty-president understanding. For example, the president of a major Eastern university (bold enough to make his own identity known if he wishes) illustrates the mood to which a president can come: "If I ever have to listen to another faculty meeting discuss freshman English requirements I shall go stark mad. They bore me stiff!" On the other hand a frequent faculty complaint is that "the president has lost any 'real appreciation for scholarship.'"

Sometimes they have tried to organize their own administrative responsibilities so that they might teach a course, or at least supervise it and give it shape. Where this could not be done they have sometimes sought to develop alter egos who would be able to do for them what their overwhelming administrative loads would not permit them to do for themselves.

One cannot help admiring these attempts (for they have been scarcely more than attempts) of able and brilliant men who were, perhaps, as much in rebellion against the intellectual confinement of college presidents as they were concerned for the improvement of education for students. Such were the efforts of Hutchins at Chicago to revise almost an entire system of educational thought and organization; of Conant at Harvard in teaching science; and, more distantly, Glenn Frank's sponsorship at Wisconsin of the Experimental College for the development of liberal education. In the academic arena their handicaps have been many, the odds against them overwhelming.[13]

Let it be said bluntly that the decline of direct presidential intervention in the intellectual activities of the college is not so regrettable as it may, at first, appear. Things have changed. Certainly few, if any, presidents can make the personal investment of time, energy, and study which effective teaching requires. He will miss too many classes. His preparation will, of necessity, frequently be skimpy and to the sharp ears of students even a president, trying to fill an hour for which he is not adequately prepared, will sound like any other faculty filibuster.

But it is in the faculty that real scepticism of direct presidential participation has its roots. Does the president think that he can do as a spare-time activity a better job than the faculty members

---

[13] I mention only these more spectacular examples to illustrate the generic problems involved, not to exclude reference to many other efforts at intellectual leadership on the part of many presidents. In some instances of happy combinations of circumstances and personalities, some presidents have been able to achieve a measure of success.

to whom such work is virtually an obsession? If his ideas on teaching and subject matter are so good why doesn't he get them accepted by the customary methods of persuasion in the academic market place rather than by resorting to administrative authority? Moreover, whatever his skills as an administrator, if he sets himself up as an example of teaching, his work can expect no immunity from the ruthless criteria to which other faculty members are subject. When the president becomes an active member of the faculty it is hard to avoid implications that are uncomplimentary to both the egotism of a president or the competence of the faculty. This is why presidential participation in, or personal programs of, actual educational operations usually survive only so long as the particular president is there to see that they do. Such activities tend to expire with the expiration of his interest or of his term of office. At best, they tend quickly to lose their identity in the general work of the faculty.

Yet what has been said about the presidents' educational leadership is less a denial of its importance than a criticism of the form it takes. Indeed, the very specialization of the faculty makes the perspective and breadth of presidential leadership in higher education more important than ever; but this is a leadership as to ends and purposes and not as to methods and subject matter. The president is in a much better position than the faculty to ask: What kind of educational product are we trying to turn out? How well are we succeeding? Are the courses we are teaching the right ones? Are there others which would be better? Is there evidence that we are producing competence? culture? morality? Are we trying to do too much? Not enough? Are there things we should stop doing, and other things we should do?

These are the questions a president must ask, but it is not his place to answer them alone. He must ask them of the faculty, insistently if he wishes, but with substantial willingness to consider their answers. Faculty members will teach effectively only what *they* believe in, not what a president tells them they should teach. His skill as an educational leader lies in uniting them in their views as to the kind of institution they all serve, why it exists at all, for whom it is trying to provide education, and what kind of education it is trying to provide. If these basic ideas are clear, if they are shared by president and faculty, if they are kept bright and resolute through constant examination and discussion, they will do more to ease the strains and release the energies of the institution than will any number of new millions in endowment.

VIII

The President and the Students

A CAMPUS is dead when its students are not there; it hums when they are. Not only are the students themselves galvanic but they galvanize everyone else—faculty, deans, presidents, and campus police. The annual return of the students inspires in everyone connected with a college the mixed feelings of a happy homecoming and the wariness of people who are compelled to live in occupied territory.

In the minds of most persons, teaching is the central and most continuing responsibility of the college. In addition to the energies which go into teaching students, however, a large part of the administrative preoccupations of every college centers around them. Their sheer numbers would make this inevitable; there are no small colleges any more. And the fact that colleges and universities are becoming complex places makes student administration necessary. The guidance, discipline, housing, and general care of students requires specialized attention from wise and experienced people who must be skillful in management and who should possess a knowledge of psychology of the young which approaches omniscience.

Every college in varying degree provides organization for discipline, dormitory management, hospital care, vocational counseling, recreation, public lectures and concerts, and extracurricular activities. Over and beyond these official provisions, the restless ingenuity and energy of college students invent and require a host of other supplementary outlets—fraternities, sororities and other social organizations, and student clubs bringing together those who have like minds about anything and everything from horses to hi-fi. Political organizations exist feebly but in numbers, and humane organizations—the Campus Chest, relief for the Chinese and Hungarians—embody generous impulses. International affairs and transient causes create discussion clubs. Over every campus broods the problem of reconciling the automobile with both education and coeducation. Finally and inescapably, there is the student newspaper.

The president's relation these days to all this shimmering organization is likely to be indirect and distant rather than direct and intimate. The modern college president, unlike his counterpart of a generation ago, no longer teaches. Frequent or compulsory chapels and convocations are rare. His contacts with the students are confined, for the most part, to ceremonial occasions such as the president's reception for the freshmen, the annual junior prom or its equivalent, and commencements. Even his personal acquaintance with students is usually limited to a relatively small number of student leaders, a contact which must be carefully handled to avoid embarrassments for himself or for them. Put bluntly, for the president students are becoming more and more just one more factor in the complex of institutional management; their education he must leave to others.

Yet not a day will pass but the president will be made conscious of student problems. In this area he presides over no sleeping volcano; it is always smoking and frequently erupts. College students are at an age when, as President Dickey of Dartmouth has said, their appetites and powers are at flood tide and when "they

THE PRESIDENT AND THE STUDENTS 131

will never again know less about what can happen!" In fact, students probably contribute more than anyone else to the general anxiety neuroses of college presidents. Usually the contributions are trivial but sometimes they are tragic; it is the uncertainty which kills. Every college president learns to scan quickly each issue of the local paper for possible references to college affairs before he even thinks of turning to any account of international crises. The paper may report only the harmless item that John Harrison, a sophomore, was arrested for speeding. It may, if the telephone has not already told him, report that John Harrison's car has wrapped itself around a tree, that the parents of Mary Montgomery must be told that she is dead, and the parents of three others notified that their children are in the hospital. Where there is much that is trivial and transient in American college life there is enough which is lingering and tragic to sober both students and administrators. I doubt that it was student administrators who started the bromide that the young keep one young.

Out of all the joint involvement between students and the college, there has emerged in the American academic organization a group of specialists in student administration. The functions of these officers vary from campus to campus. In general they include deans of men and of women, deans of students, house directors, student counselors, social directors, recreation advisors, and nurses and doctors in student infirmaries.

Without any thought of disparagement it can be said that one whole phase of student life is a kind of continuing soap opera. No president could possibly cope with the variety of matters which have to be dealt with without the help of these trained and conscientious assistants. They are indispensable. Perhaps it should be said gently that because it is indispensable, student personnel administration has become something of a cult in its own right with, sometimes, resulting confusion as to whether students are primarily in college to be taken care of or to get an education. At any rate, the president's life is longer and infinitely easier because the student personnel experts are there.

The most important fact about the student when he finally reaches the college campus is that he has been reared in what the professional educators call a "child-centered" society. I shall not attempt a social or psychological analysis of what has produced such a society or what its characteristics are, but the fact that ours is such seems undeniable. I suppose parents in all times and places have loved their children, but I doubt whether the anthropologists can find any other society in which, directly and indirectly, children are the object of so much privilege and special attention as they are in America. Concern about their education, their morals, their health, their recreation, their working conditions, their freedom of expression, and their protection from the unseemly has, so far as I know, no counterpart elsewhere in the world. Moreover, the child, as a future college student, has flourished in an atmosphere which the social psychologist has insisted should be maintained as much or more for him than for his parents. "Child-controlled" is a phrase with meaning in America.

The education of the average college freshman has been acquired throughout the grades and high school fairly painlessly. His grades have been high; the emphasis has been upon reward for success, rarely penalty for failure. The intellectual demand generally has not been strenuous, fitted as it was into a welter of outside activities and requiring little homework. The distinction between academic study and nonacademic activity has been so badly blurred that the student has an impression that everything he does is "educational" whether it is practicing for the senior play, reading history, or going out for track, and that all of these expenditures of time are about equally valuable.

This background naturally reflects itself in the personality of the college student and the student's approach to college study. The American student invades the realm of ideas as his pioneer ancestors took possession of the country—as if no one had ever been there before. He respects no claims marked out by Plato, Rousseau, Euclid, or Newton. No authority awes him. He is not so much interested in learning what others before him have thought as in learning whether they agree with him, or he with them. His sense of history is slight because he has always lived in a society which is preoccupied with the present and the future, not with the past. He is ready to agree with Jefferson that the earth belongs to the living. He is much more interested in what the country will be like in 1975 than what it was like in 1775. He is only mildly curious about abstract ideas because all his life he has been surrounded by concrete and specific things which moved and occupied space. He has been conditioned by all his newspapers and magazines to a factual interest in life: what is useful, what will work, how much it costs, how it can be changed. He has moved so often from place to place with his family, watched the annual changes in cars and fashions, and seen so many elections that the acceptance of change is "built in"—the *status quo* is something to be preserved only as long as it is serviceable. He has been conditioned to a healthy respect for his own ideas—he has been encouraged to express them at home and in school. He takes democracy seriously; one man's opinion is as good as another's, and this includes his own opinion, too.

This, then, is the kind of young person who stares back at the college president at opening convocation, a person as sensitive as a radio receiver to every kind of radiant impulse in the atmosphere, and just about as selective. Whatever is broadcast on his wave length, he receives. It is wrong to call the American college student anti-intellectual; he is merely anti-pedantic, just as is the society which produces him. Learning must prove its claims to his attention. To do so it must prove itself interesting and useful— and be quick about it. When it does, he responds eagerly, even if not fanatically. Like Socrates long before him he has little patience with learning for its own sake, for the sake of ornament or even of self-enjoyment. He finds there are many ways to discover pleasure, and to the average college student, study for its own sake is one of the minor ones. Let the subject be interesting, let it show its relationship to the world already being formed in his mind, let the professor and the student be persons between whom a common understanding can be reached: the result goes far to explain the vibrant quality of American college campuses.

If this is something of what the president sees at the opening convocation of college, perhaps the students should also look closely at the president. It may be that hereafter they will see no more of him than he will see of them. In some of our major institutions the opening exercises may be the students' last glimpse of the president until commencement, four years hence.

The reason for the separation of the president and the students is that in all our colleges, administration has claimed the president for its own; and there is much distance and many people between him and the students. He is keenly aware that he presides over an institution in which he and his colleagues have been straining every nerve to make these students comfortable, to look after their health, to counsel them, to entertain them, and to give them the best possible education at the lowest possible cost. Yet, their actual education, what these students learn and how well they learn it, is only indirectly his responsibility. The pleasures and pains of learning belong to faculty-student association; the president's satisfactions must come from providing the means of education—the best faculty he can hire, the best library, the best classrooms, and the best laboratories he can provide. The division of educational labor makes the students not so much a personal intellectual concern of the president as it makes them one more component of management—a most important component—affecting his problems of public relations, of money raising, and of internal administration.

THE PRESIDENT AND THE STUDENTS

How students have evolved more and more into a factor of management for the president may perhaps be most dramatically (but not exclusively) illustrated in the experience of publicly supported schools. Every president of a state college knows that his ability to coax money from the public is directly related to the size of the student body—the more students, the more money; the fewer students, the less money. Numbers are the president's most potent arguments; quality and function in education are facts much harder for the public to appreciate. For the presidents of private institutions the problem may actually be the same or it may merely take a different form. If the private college is crucially dependent for its support on student fees, the recruitment and retention of students must always be a major presidential worry. If the institution limits its enrollment and is wealthy enough to be relatively independent of student income, the worry becomes one of selection—not how many, but whether the *right* students have been attracted, admitted, and retained.[1] The temptation for administrators therefore to see students not so much as educational responsibilities as problems of institutional management is subtle and powerful.

The president now almost never sees students in the classrooms. If he sees them at all, it is usually under circumstances which involve social or administrative duties—fraternity and sorority dinners, football games, social visits to the residence halls, public lectures or concerts, student delegations bringing him petitions or complaints. Unconsciously, the president comes to think of students in other than educational terms, as pipelines to parents, as future alumni whose support the college will need, as sources of income, as insatiable objects of expenditure, and as a potential public relations instrument more dangerous or more useful than

[1] This factor is well illustrated by the anxieties of some of our most famous Eastern colleges, which are eager to develop national rather than regional enrollments.

almost any other. No matter how warm he may feel toward students in the abstract, he develops a wary reserve toward them in the concrete, for they have a way of enormously complicating life for him. No amount of sentimental attachment to youth can quite displace an uneasy presidential instinct against ambush.

Today most of his contacts with students arise, as has been pointed out, not out of the education of students but out of their activities and out of administrative responsibility for their general welfare. Unconsciously, the nonacademic interests of students become identified with the "administration," while their intellectual interests become identified with the faculty. Between study and campus activities there is always a tug of war. Since administration and faculty each seek eagerly to do in their respective ways all they can for students, the tug of war appears at times to be between the administration at one end and the faculty at the other. It is, of course, a conflict which no college president would care openly to admit and would prefer to conceal or to deny; but it is nevertheless inherent in the present division of educational responsibility. The students look to the faculty for instruction; they look to the administration for the origin, encouragement, and regulation of the noninstructional aspects of college life. It is these aspects which insist upon more and more attention. In this relation to campus activities one gets the best insight into the president's relation to the students. The extracurricular side of college going deserves here a little more discussion.

Going to college is, for an American student, a social as well as an intellectual event. It is sometimes difficult to tell which set of interests is dominant. The colleges in general not only accept this fact but also accommodate themselves to it. They even create the conditions of life on their campuses which encourage a great deal of the excitement which contributes so much to the pleasure and perhaps even to the education of students, although not particularly to their intellectual development. The conditions of resident living, fraternities and sororities, organized intramural and intercollegiate athletics, the diversions which accompany coeducation, and even the fact of student employment, so characteristic of American colleges, all of these contribute to the exhilarating variety of college life.

In their efforts to adjust to each other, both the students and the colleges make many mutual accommodations. A freshman finds himself under considerably greater educational pressure than he has felt before; he begins to understand that "trying hard" is no substitute for success, that the mastery of knowledge has little to do with the likes and dislikes of the learner, that generous teachers cannot excuse him from the requirements which competence demands. These things, at the outset, he may not clearly understand and they may be disturbing, resulting in low grades, emotional distress, and possible failure.

But if the college hits the freshman hard, let it be said that the freshman also hits the college hard. It is an interesting question as to which influences the other more. The students, remember, have been previously conditioned by "child-centered" schools and home life. This focus cannot be suddenly abandoned. The college cannot educate students, it cannot even keep them in school, unless the demands it makes upon them are somewhat accommodated to what they are able to learn. If the students are not well prepared when they come, the colleges must offer them more preparatory work, especially in such fields as chemistry, languages, and mathematics. In freshman courses much high school material is repeated, sometimes greatly to the disappointment and boredom of the brighter freshmen. The development of teaching aids, of textbooks with "popular" appeal, the emphasis on courses, on specific assignments, and even upon good teaching, all contribute their share to an institutional feeling among both faculty and students that it is the responsibility of the college to do everything it can to make the student's education as simple and as attractive as possible. Educators debate as an open question: When students fail, is it the fault of the student or of the college?

All of this develops a sense of expectation on the part of the student and a habit of accommodation on the part of the college. These take many forms and have many consequences. The administrative efforts to take into consideration the wishes, comfort, and convenience of students naturally arouse the expectation in students' minds that their wishes, comfort, and convenience in matters of their instruction will also be considered. To these expectations the faculty and administration do accommodate themselves—sometimes, to be sure, with much huffing and puffing but making genuine concessions nonetheless. It is unpopular to say so (and the fact that it is unpopular is itself significant) but there is much about college life which prolongs the immaturity of the student. In almost every phase of his life there is someone to advise him about his program or about his personal problems, to help him with scholarships or with loans, to keep him out of trouble, or to rescue him if he gets into it. Gradually the student comes to believe that this institution is *his;* that everyone wants to do something for him; and to keep this wonderful arrangement operating in his favor it is necessary to exert himself only in moderation.

This focus upon the student as the center around which the institution arranges itself frequently receives administrative or official recognition.[2] The students may be asked to rate their professors, encouraged to publish their opinions in the papers, pass judgment upon college management. They feel it their province to put college officials through examinations about the institution's

[2] The public relations officers in their promotional literature about college life usually emphasize this primacy of the student. Even when not said explicitly, the impression is created that the college exists only for the student —a very limited conception.

affairs. In some schools, students have actually been invited to participate in management, to sit as members of official committees, and even to manage property. In a few universities—North Carolina, Washington, California, and some others—students have even been organized as corporations and have been put officially in charge of athletics, bookstores, or other enterprises. Actual control in all of these instances is more nominal than real.[3]

These characteristics of American college life have long been the subject of educational discussions, serious and satirical, here and abroad. The characteristics, however, must be accepted; efforts to change them have met with no particular success. The democracy of American education, its vocational and practical tradition, the age and social conditioning of college students, the absence of a tradition of learning, the dominant pattern of coeducation, the widespread view that all activity is "educational," and the particular philosophy of service which dominates our colleges, these are the foundations on which college going in this country rests. And, it should be added, greatly to the credit of the American college, its contributions to the social life of the country are far greater and more varied than if its activities were confined to purely intellectual interests. The problem on the American campus is to secure and maintain a balance of interests.

Many a college president has been puzzled and fretful at his inability to arrest the steady encroachment of nonacademic interests upon the time of students and faculty, upon the college budget, and upon his own time and energy. Yet most efforts to

[3] The *pro forma,* almost deceptive, character of these types of "student control" gradually becomes evident to each succeeding generation of students about the time it leaves the campus, thus contributing to their cynicism or to campus turmoil. The following quotation from one of the student newspapers plaintively reflects the student bewilderment about their ambiguous position. "We would, however, ask this of the Administration: If extracurricular activities are really out of the hands of the students, please don't tell us otherwise. Don't consult us in one breath and try to fool us in the next. We shall learn to live with our fate. But, please tell us the truth."

restrict such activities have met with failure. Long ago, Woodrow Wilson observed that the sideshows at Princeton were threatening to replace the main tent, but his attempts to reverse the process brought a warning from one of the alumni that Wilson was threatening to make the college "a damned institution of learning." It should be noted that Wilson failed when he attacked the club system—the local equivalent of fraternities—of Princeton.

Perhaps the most successful attack on what he called the "trivialization" of college life was made by President Hutchins at the University of Chicago. But in some respects it was a Pyrrhic victory and its success largely disappeared with his own administration. Colleges which run counter to the national traditions do so at their peril. Many which have experimented with genuine deviations have found themselves cut off from students and from popular support and understanding. The factors which hold American colleges and universities in their orbits make really daring departures dangerous and difficult.

Nevertheless, to a college president the presence on the campus of nonacademic activities in such profusion presents serious problems. The question is not whether he will stamp out such activities —this would be too negative an accomplishment, even if it were possible; rather, the question is where the president will take his own stand, as to which of the numerous forces contending for dominance on the campus he will encourage—those of educational demand or those of institutional accommodation. The spirit, and eventually many of the practices, of the college will reflect his personal attitude.

Actually, the influence of the president on the educational atmosphere of the campus is less the product of deliberate decision than it is the consequence of personal expression and conduct in the daily administration of his responsibilities. Every president verbally supports the intellectual interests of the campus but his

THE PRESIDENT AND THE STUDENTS

administration, without his quite knowing it, can lend support to the opposite forces. It is easy to see how this may happen.

The president, for example, knows that all administrative affairs of the college, its relationships to parents and alumni, the management of its dormitories, its attractiveness to future students, and even its financial affairs are much more easily managed if the present crop of students is pleased rather than disgruntled. People, especially young people, are pleased if they get what they want (or what they think they want); hence it is tempting to the president to see that the students, insofar as he can insure it, get what they want. This administrative eagerness to please, conveyed by a thousand gestures of concern for student welfare and opinion, means inevitably tolerance of, if not actual encouragement to, the nonintellectual aspects of campus life; for the youthfulness and the inexperience of students will often lead them to prefer the diversions of college life to its main purpose. To put the matter bluntly, the more nearly the education of students becomes for the president a "paper" concern, a matter of finance, of public relations, and of impersonal administration, the greater is his temptation to "manage" the students so that they will contribute most to and detract least from the efficient (meaning undisturbed) operation of the college.

Evidence as to what campus interests the president supports quickly accumulates. It accumulates from his relations with students, where sometimes he may youthfully identify himself with their activities, join in the rallies, the yells, wear the freshman hat. The students may get the impression that he is one of them if he is readily available to student photographers, calls the student leaders by their first names, and even permits them to call him by his. He adds further to the evidence by the kinds of groups he generally addresses and by what he says to them. If he seldom attends concerts, but never misses a football game; if he goes to the junior prom, but rarely to faculty lectures; if he advocates the construction of a stadium before the library is built, both the students and the faculty will sense the character of his basic concerns and will take their cues.

If, on the other hand, his talks to students are about intellectual interests, designed more to inform or stimulate than to entertain; if he supports the disciplinary officers of the college in the even-handed administration of justice regardless of what students are affected; if he makes clear that in complaints about the faculty the student bears the burden of proof, it will be equally clear the president is in fact, as well as in word, on the side of intellectual demand. Such a president provides, in a word, leadership.

The president, however, who attempts such educational leadership will find himself pretty constantly embroiled. The reasons for his difficulty are traceable to a widespread misconception of what colleges and universities are really for. In our society, there is a tendency to believe that institutions of higher education are merely service institutions, whose duty it is to provide the kind of education which the students prefer or which the public is willing to support. This view may be essentially true of elementary and secondary schools, where "education for citizenship" is certainly an important part of the service they perform. The public, of course, may determine the kind of education it wants for citizenship, and to what extent it wishes to have universal literacy. *But neither the wishes of students nor those of the public determine the nature of higher education.*

The nature of higher education is determined by its fundamental mission, namely, to discover and to teach the truth. Whatever this mission requires in the way of devotion, of freedom, or of financial support must be provided if the mission is to be accomplished. The public has the privilege of refusing to support its institutions of higher education, but in so doing the public is merely deciding that it is content with less knowledge than it might otherwise have. Truth, so to speak, may be had only on its own terms. The village which voted that the world was flat did not affect the curvature of the earth. Neither students nor the public are required to devote themselves to learning. But their refusal to do so means that they must pay the penalities for ignorance.

No one has stated the tyrannical requirements of learning more forcefully than Thomas H. Huxley:

> Suppose it were perfectly certain that the life and fortune of every one of us would, one day or other, depend upon his winning or losing a game of chess. Don't you think that we should all consider it to be a primary duty to learn at least the names and the moves of the pieces; to have a notion of a gambit, and a keen eye for all the means of giving and getting out of check? Do you not think that we should look with a disapprobation amounting to scorn, upon the father who allowed his son, or the state which allowed its members, to grow up without knowing a pawn from a knight?
>
> Yet it is a very plain and elementary truth, that the life, the fortune, and the happiness of every one of us, and, more or less, of those who are connected with us, do depend upon our knowing something of the rules of a game infinitely more difficult and complicated than chess. It is a game which has been played for untold ages, every man and woman of us being one of the two players in a game of his or her own. The chessboard is the world, the pieces are the phenomena of the universe, the rules of the game are what we call the laws of Nature. The player on the other side is hidden from us. We know that his play is always fair, just, and patient. But also we know, to our cost, that he never overlooks a mistake, or makes the smallest allowance for ignorance. To the man who plays well, the highest stakes are paid, with that sort of overflowing generosity with which the strong shows delight in strength. And one who plays ill is checkmated—without haste, but without remorse.[4]

In heightening the appreciation of students, faculty, administration, and the public for this "demand" quality of higher education, the college president performs one of his greatest services.

[4] Thomas H. Huxley, *A Liberal Education: Autobiography and Selected Essays*, edited by A. L. F. Snell (Boston: 1909), pp. 39–40.

Yet too often his weight is thrown in the other direction. With an eye to student popularity, the approval of parents, for superficial public attention, or merely from intellectual slackness, the president announces that "the university lives only for its students." Such pronouncements add to the confusion and to the misunderstandings about the nature of universities. How much more accurate to say, not that the university exists for the student, but that the student has come to the university to enlist in a cause and to prepare to serve it, the cause for which the university itself exists—the search for truth.

Colleges and universities do not "live for students"; they can do little for their students unless those students are enlisted in the same cause which the institutions serve, and unless the students submit themselves to the same discipline. Colleges and universities exist not to serve students but to wage war against ignorance; what army was ever organized merely to serve its recruits?

The notion that a college can be whatever the students, faculty, administration, or public may want it to be is a curious and serious error—and held by far too many people. If a college or university is an institution devoted to discovering and teaching the truth, it ceases to be such an institution unless the students, faculty, and administration *meet the conditions which the mission requires*. To the extent that the conditions are not met, whether by irrelevant and distracting student activities, by incompetent or indifferent faculty or administrators, or by the restrictions of public support or opinion, to that extent the institution is something less of a college or university than it might be.

This is why it is important that the president attempt not necessarily to transform the traditional conditions of college life, but to make his own position and relationship to them clear and to explain to the students the nature of the institution which they are attending. Whatever his inclinations, he cannot remove from student life in America the distractions which actually limit education; but he can discourage them. As the price of such action, he will forfeit some claims to immediate popularity, but he will advance his claims to lasting respect. Which he prefers is a test of his own character.

IX

The Uneasy Campus

Among people outside the colleges and universities there is a fairly widespread impression that, while it may not be the road to riches, the academic life is ideal. A pleasant campus, an interesting world of books and ideas, an atmosphere of leisure, and the association of like-minded people contribute to the belief that this should be as close to an earthly paradise as men are privileged to come. In euphoric moments college professors have been known to say that they get paid for doing what they would want to do anyway.

Yet those who choose college work or drift into it soon discover that there is much illusion about its peace, that it has its own brands of stresses and strains. Whether these are more or less intense than those of other professions it may be impossible to judge; those in the academic world regard their own crosses as sufficiently heavy. Indeed, despite the favorable factors of academic life, its strains are revealed in nervous breakdowns, distorted personalities, frustrations, disappointments, and conflicts. These are too evident and too abundant to be ignored in any review of higher education, and particularly in any examination of the problems of the college president.

The tensions in higher education are, in general, of three kinds. The first are those which are inherent in intellectual work. The second arise from the organization, activities, and limitations of faculties and faculty members. The third grow out of the relations between faculties and administrations. While it is the tensions of the third category which are the principal responsibility of the college president, all the categories are actually inextricable.

Teaching is itself a peculiar profession, historically and inherently beset with paradoxes. It has been extolled in the most extravagant terms—"the teacher," even the unsentimental Henry Adams said, "affects eternity"—yet from the earliest times our Western societies have caricatured teachers as slightly ridiculous people. There is no doubt that teachers are indispensable to the continuation and improvement of our stage of civilization but other professions have generally been given greater respect and higher rewards. Teaching, viewed from one angle, requires an egotism that amounts almost to effrontery—the intention to shape the minds and personalities of others according to a pattern of one's own. Yet more than other professions, teaching attracts a large proportion of thoughtful, introspective, unaggressive people. The longer one is associated with teaching and with teachers, the larger loom the mysteries of both.[1]

The college professor lives in an intellectually frustrating world. For him there are no final answers, no authorities which

---

[1] It is quite probable that teaching as an activity (as distinguished from an interest in the subject-matter taught) is not itself a completely self-sustaining interest. There is considerable evidence that its vitality coincides with the biological span of family-rearing. This may account for the fact that so many teachers "go dead" in their fifties, bored with the strenuous and unnatural task of continuing to help the young. It is here that diversionary interests in research and administration can help to make the task of teaching more tolerable, can help the teacher cope with the problems of his own personal and intellectual evolution. The problem is more serious for the elementary and high schools because the possibilities of diluting the task of the teacher in those schools with supplementary activities is more difficult than it is in the colleges and universities.

are not open to question. There are no adequate explanations: he is merely the agent for presenting the best explanations we have. No sooner is history written than it must be rewritten; the readers are new. No interpretation of literature suffices very long. Even when facts remain the same, interest changes. In a sense, no matter what intellectual battles the college professor wins—the books written, the brilliant students trained, the reputation made—the victories are temporary, soon remembered only as skirmishes in the onward movement of the continuing war on ignorance.[2]

Such a world is full of strain. It is a world of perpetual perplexity, in which there is no rest. No one who has not lived in it can fully understand it. Its tasks, like woman's work, are never done, and it is this haunting sense of "the little done, the undone vast" which keeps the college professor from being comfortable even when he is happy. William James said toward the close of his career that if he had it to do over again he would seek more satisfaction from doing the work than from the results of the work done.

This ceaseless pursuit of knowledge has its satisfactions, of course, and to some people these satisfactions are sufficient in themselves; to be left alone to teach, to study, to travel without thought of arrival is happiness enough. But in our society such selfless, scholarly spirits are rare and are becoming rarer. The college professor has, in common with others, the craving for status, good living, and a desire to share in what his generation feels is most significant. Unhappily his profession is not as good an avenue to these ends as he might often wish. It is, for example, paid less well. Moreover, society gives its accolades not to men of thought but to men of power and action. The quest for these

[2] When J. Robert Oppenheimer was asked how he would define a scientific advance, he replied that it was something which one's professional colleagues welcomed, *i.e.*, needed. In addition to its other implications, the reply explains why discoveries are less important for the data they contain than they are as instruments of further advancement.

personal satisfactions—for "success"—in the academic world is limited to fewer forms and outlets than in many other fields, and the resulting crowded striving helps to account for the tensions and conflicts which arise from faculty organizations and activities.

The quest for reputation and power is to be found in the college and university much as it is in other organizations. Perhaps, indeed, the very limitations of the forms of success available to the teachers and scholar make the rivalries keener.[3] Academic reputation, pursued particularly through the medium of scholarly publication, has become a goal of fierce competitive endeavor. Teaching, as a road to distinction or to national reputation, is now very difficult, confined as it must be to a relatively small proportion of the students of even a small college. One's words disappear with the students' memories. Publication, however, offers more: a claim upon the attention of students and of professional colleagues everywhere, a permanent record of one's work, a clear basis on which one may be compared and judged. Publication is the certificate of admission to the lists of the academic tournament. Quite aside from the vast contributions to knowledge that the passion for publication has brought about, it has become an increasingly powerful compulsion in higher education, particularly in the universities. This is especially true where promotions, salary increases, and tenure have come to be closely linked with publication records.

The anxieties resulting from these forms of competition for individual recognition and advancement can be very intense.[4]

---

[3] Woodrow Wilson once remarked that he had never learned anything about politics after he left Princeton!

[4] William H. Whyte, Jr., in his provocative book, *The Organization Man* (New York: Simon and Schuster, 1956), p. 153, has made some interesting comparisons between different professional groups as to the forms and relative intensities of their internal rivalries. Most people seem to believe that the strains of competition within their own professional group are more intense than are those in any other. "Let me add a personal testimonial on this score. Comparatively speaking, of all the kinds of people I have come

Some professors are much more effective competitors than others; they are sometimes able, through the skillful acquisition of research funds and the use of graduate students and aides, to make themselves veritable production lines. Others, tormented by a spirit of perfectionism, simply cannot produce and look upon their work as a creative art not to be turned out on order. Still others, for a variety of reasons, resent the pressure for publication and grow critical of administration and of compliant colleagues, both of whom they hold responsible for their own discomfort. Criticism, jealousy, and departmental feuds between those who do publish and those who do not occur with unhappy frequency. Each group finds it easy to classify the other disparagingly as "young squirts" or "dead wood."[5]

One stage above the rivalries for individual recognition are the faculty rivalries for a place in the sun for their respective subjects or fields of study. The striving may be for a place for a latecomer to the curriculum—geophysics, for example—or for a new status as an institute or school or even a separate college for some already well-established study. It may take the form of competition for more of the students' time, or for more students—a battle to achieve a required rather than an elective status in the

---

in contact with, corporation men have seemed to me the least given to backbiting and personal animadversions. Most of the popular novels, movies, and plays on the subject give a quite contrary impression, but I think this is due to failure to distinguish between the entrepreneur and the organization man. The businessmen who draw popular attention are apt to be entrepreneurs who, like Robert Young, exist on strife and are never so happy as when they are publicly reviling their enemies. The corporation man is a different breed; he has obeyed the precept to team play so long it has become part of his personality. One result is often a rather automatic, icy, bonhomie, but another is a remarkable capacity to disagree with colleagues professionally without having to dislike them personally. *By contrast, the academic and literary worlds often seem like a jungle.*" (Italics mine.)

[5] One of the more scathing exposés of the pettiness which academic rivalry can engender is to be found in R. L. Warren, "Weapons of the Weak," *American Association of University Professors Bulletin*, December 1941, pp. 557–567.

college curriculum. The competition may be for a larger part of the budget, or preferred salary treatment for the members of a currently favored department, or for additional staff, or for a new building. In all of these forms of striving, the sense of strain can affect the morale of an entire institution and can even be a force in molding individual personalities.

While the intellectual life breeds its own tensions for the individual, and faculty organization and activities create a special brand of strain, the campus conflicts with which we are here most concerned are those which arise from the relations between the faculty and the president. Although eased here and there by special circumstances or by the soothing solvent of unusual personalities, conflicts between faculty and administration or, at least, a large measure of self-consciousness between them, exist noticeably in almost all institutions of higher learning. Why should this be true? The answer lies in a combination of factors, not all of the same nature or order of importance, ranging from the philosophical—the eternal conflict between freedom and authority—to such concrete matters as salary and protocol.

Before some of the specific causes of academic friction are examined, one other generic factor which intensifies every form of campus tension must be mentioned. This is the growth of academic bureaucracy: the multiplication of routines, organization, and machinery essential, on the one hand, to the management of large enterprise and, on the other, paralyzing to its spirit. The organization of the academic year into semesters and quarters and of courses into credit hours, the calculation of teaching loads, the preoccupation of faculty members with endless forms and reports involving grades and registration, majors, minors, transfers, student advising, withholding taxes, faculty meetings, and committees breed states of mind far removed from either scholarship or teaching.

To the faculty mind, the campus bureaucracy is a kind of trap which confines but does not kill. Admittedly the volume and complexity of academic business require organization, and organization exalts routines and standardization. It represses spontaneity. The factory-feeling creeps on the campus. Furthermore, the growth of bureaucracy multiplies offices and officers within both faculty and nonfaculty. It establishes and hardens authority and status, with resulting concern about protocol and administrative channels. With status grows privilege—a reserved parking place for the administrator, the right of the senior faculty member to teach what he wishes at his chosen hour, as against the necessity for the junior instructor to teach what he must when it is assigned.

It is easy to inveigh against the frustrations of bureaucracy and to denounce its incompatibility with the spirit of learning; it is something else to do anything effective about it. The institutional loads exist and grow heavier and they cannot be carried without organization. With organization inevitably come discipline and restraint. With restraint come restiveness and a blind, habitual querulousness which can be quite undiscriminating. If, as it has been defined, freedom is a knowledge of necessity, the academic world still has much to learn about reconciling the bureaucracy of its new, diverse, and heavier responsibilities with its necessary freedom.[6]

Perhaps, as has been said, the fundamental source of conflict grows out of the fact that as colleges have come to require more and more management, administrators and faculties have grown

[6] Veblen denounced academic bureaucracy as the vampire of the spirit of learning. His analysis still inspires a response in the rebellious minds of weary faculty. But his solution, boiled down, is that we ought not to have the kinds of colleges and universities we have, i.e., with large numbers of undergraduates. This suggestion is obviously of no help. *The Higher Learning in America*, ch. 3 (New York: Huebsch, 1918). An article by Charles H. Page, "Bureaucracy and Higher Education," *Journal of General Education*, V, January 1951, pp. 91–100, is at once a thoughtful analysis of the problem and an interesting example of faculty irritation with its insolubility.

farther apart. Few deans and fewer presidents ever teach any more, while faculties grow more obsessed with the increasing demands of their fields, with their scholarship, and with their research. The distinction between administration and instruction is difficult to define but the distinction is important; in general, administration is occupied with matters of organization and management, the faculty with instruction. The faculty is concerned with what, educationally, is being done, the administration with the ways and means of doing it. While ideally these activities are inseparable, they do in fact become separated when they are vested in different persons who are exclusively occupied with their own particular division of labor.

One may state this basic cleavage another way: the faculty tends to think of everything in terms of the effect on its own educational work of instruction or research. The president tends to think of everything in terms of its effect upon the reputation, the development, and the potential of the institution. Again one may say, there should ideally be no conflict here but there is, and it steadily grows more intense. What is required from a faculty point of view to make a field of academic work flourish may not be at all what is required from a president's point of view to make a college or university flourish. The problems of the college of whatever nature, from academic freedom to the parking of automobiles, will often find administrators and faculty with quite different centers of loyalty and concern. The faculty wants all issues resolved on "principle" as if the particular situation were detachable from everything else; the administration wants to settle nothing until its effect upon the fortunes and the future development of the institution can be assessed.

A classic case of the difference of viewpoint between administration and faculty will suffice to illustrate a hundred more recent ones. Professor Edward W. Bemus, a young economist at the

University of Chicago, made a speech against the railroad companies during the bitter Pullman strike of 1893. He declared:

If the railroads would expect their men to be law-abiding, they must set the example. Let their open violation of the interstate commerce law and their relations to corrupt legislatures and assessors testify as to their past in this regard. Let there be some equality in the treatment of these things.

The reaction to these mild statements was swift. President Harper of the University of Chicago wrote Bemus:

Your speech has caused me a great deal of annoyance. It is hardly safe for me to venture into any of the Chicago clubs. I am pounced upon from all sides. I propose that in the remainder of your connection with the university, you exercise very great care in public utterance about questions that are agitating the minds of the people.[7]

Without reference to the merits of the controversy, the remarks of both reveal the dominant and frequntly different concerns of faculty members and administrators and indicate an inevitable source of strain between them. For Bemus, the Pullman strike was an economic and social matter and as an economist he felt an obligation to analyze it as objectively as he could and to discuss it as a part of his moral obligation to present the truth. To President Harper, the necessity for discussing the Pullman strike as an economic and social matter was distinctly less important than were the care and preservation of the University of Chicago, and any discussion of it which threatened the welfare, as he saw it, of the University, was out of place and dangerous. Bemus certainly was not indifferent to the welfare of the University, nor was Harper indifferent to the claims of justice. But the preoccupations of each related them to the University with quite different and, practically, irreconcilable interests.

[7] This incident is reported in R. Hofstadter and W. P. Metzger, *The Development of Academic Freedom in the United States* (New York: Columbia University Press, 1955), pp. 427–428.

The college president's concern is the institution; the concern of the faculty is the care of a field of knowledge of which they are the trustees. Insofar as there are strain and conflict between the care and nurture of the institution and that of the development of the field of knowledge, there will be strain and conflict between presidents and faculties.

This basic difference between the demands of institutionalism on the one hand and the needs of freedom on the other is found in trace amounts in almost all aspects of college operation. The faculty is inclined to see an expenditure for improving the campus as nothing more than a diversion of funds which might better be spent to raise faculty salaries or buy new laboratory equipment. A new administrative assistant for the president or for the business office means to the faculty member a reduction of work for those officers whose functions seem to him intrinsically less important than his own, while his own load remains the same and his personal hopes and aspirations go unrealized. To the president, these expenditures are investments which may return to the college much more than they cost, or at least they are compromises which cost less than other alternatives which might otherwise be forced upon him. The view of each gradually becomes crystallized into a habit of looking at things which is automatically evoked when administration and faculty come into contact.

Some mutual understanding of the viewpoints of each can certainly be brought about through discussion and a widening of experience, but the conflict is inherent in the relationship of freedom to institutional necessities of management and social conformity. The forms of the conflict change but the issue remains the same. College presidents invented the basic conflict no more than did faculties; but it is safe to say that both must to a considerable degree continue to live with it.

While I am at last willing to admit that there is a residue of conflict between faculty and administration which is irreconcilable, there are nevertheless many important sources of strain which can be identified and about which something can be done. One of the outstanding sources of trouble is a lack of clear definition of authority in institutions of higher education. This is a very widespread phenomenon in American colleages and universities. Despite handbooks, codes, and mountains of faculty minutes, board records, and surveys, faculties and administrators constantly run afoul of jurisdictional areas claimed by the other. The reason is that in the academic world, authority is defined by tradition, precedent, and personalities, as well as by codes. For example, an office in the hands of one administrator is an orderly, restrained administrative operation; in the hands of another, it becomes a rapidly growing empire, characterized by border alarums and excursions. Bulwarks of authority are never proof against the impulses and programs of newly appointed administrators and staff members. At a faculty meeting shortly after Eliot's appointment as president of Harvard, an irate faculty member inquired of him, "Sir, why are there all these disturbances in the life of the college?," to which Eliot calmly replied, "I can tell you quite simply, sir. Harvard has a new president." Since the courses and orbits of administrators and faculties are not firmly described, they represent for each other errant forces whose movements are unpredictable. The result is that each in relation to the other becomes wary and mutually uneasy.

A second major source of tension is the exaltation of administration above other educational activities. The aggrandizement of the executive person in American life is a widespread phenomenon; in education, it represents for a faculty a philosophical inversion of values. It makes a master of the servant. The exaltation of the administrator gives respect and prestige to the "wrong" people and to the "wrong" functions and, in so doing, by implication denies these rights to those to whom they properly belong. It exalts legal authority above intellectual and professional authority by giving the administrator, armed with legal power only, control over the scholar, armed with wisdom and knowledge. It somehow suggests that police power is superior to the power of thought.

In addition to this philosophical affront, the practical effects are even more galling. The administrator receives the honors, privileges, and salary which faculties feel are out of keeping with the secondary importance of the function he performs. That these rewards should go to administrators indicates by contrast a low evaluation of faculty activities, with consequent faculty discontent. Thus the administrator, and particularly the president, tends to be set still farther apart, with resulting damage to institutional unity, to the freedom of communication, and to the development of understanding.

Still another source of strain between faculties and presidents arises out of the present practices involved in the selection of administrators. For members of the faculty, the ladder of promotion is clear. Progress from instructor to full professor takes place by identifiable steps related to competence and to accomplishment. The reasons for the appointment of administrators are frequently much less clear. Too often such appointments seem arbitrary, sudden, and made on the basis of unknown factors. Personal relations and personal acquaintance appear to play an important part, and no established type of either training or experience seems to govern administrative selections. Consequently, to the faculty there appear to be unknown and unpredictable forces affecting the operation of the institution which may at any time change administrative relationships and even educational policies by merely changing administrators. Uncertainty creates uneasiness, and while the faculty may be seriously affected by the choice of an administrator, a president may exercise his right to make administrative appointments with little or no faculty consultation.

Another set of factors which create administration-faculty tension may be summarized as the pathology of administration.

Authority has its effect upon people, both upon those who exercise it and those upon whom it is exercised. The president or other administrator who continues long in office undergoes changes in manner and personality, as do those, in turn, who are subject to his authority. These changes frequently result in discomfort and conflict. Sometimes the administrator becomes impatient and dictatorial; sometimes his genuine regard for the feelings of those under him or his anxious desire for their approval may make him tentative and indecisive; sometimes the variety of masters he serves may erode his own integrity and candor. Not infrequently, a college president acquires a proprietary attitude. Things become his—he speaks of "my faculty," "my board of trustees," "my buildings," "my campus"—and when he does it is more than a little galling to sensitive people to find themselves regarded as a part of an administrator's chattels.

A faculty in turn develops its own ways of countering these pathological forms of distasteful administration. Educational proposals from the president will frequently meet with coolness, if not ridicule, as invasions of faculty prerogatives. Faculty committees can make reports in which ill-disguised barbs are imbedded. Official social functions can be sparsely attended and painfully enjoyed. A few of the older, more secure professors may speak out gently about the good old days, or caustically about the dangerous effects of new administrative policies. Usually the friction, hot and smoldering, is not permitted to break into open flame; when it does, parts of the machine must almost always be replaced.

How much of all this conflict is inevitable and how much is avoidable? How much is inherent in the nature of organization itself—the necessity for superiority and subordination, the divisions of labor, the disabilities of sheer size, faulty structure? How much is due to problems of personality, to ineptness, to inexperience? How much is due to the nature of the profession itself, to faculty overwork and underpay? In what specific fields, activities, or departments does strain most frequently arise?[8] These are questions which every college president faces. What can he do to answer them?

Some things can, of course, be done about many of the sources of conflict, and a conscientious president will do them. Simplicity of organization, clarity of authority, identification of responsibility: these are matters which must have constant attention. Boredom and overwork can be countered by institutional provisions for sabbatical leaves, by occasional variations in teaching loads, by specific encouragement to research. The appointment, use, and proper support of committees can be a rewarding investment of time for the president, not only for the help they will be to the college and to him, but for their value in channeling faculty restiveness, in giving and getting information, and in providing an outlet for valuable talents and energies unabsorbed in teaching and scholarship.

The president will watch his "manners," the actual techniques of exercising his authority. His letters will be written with care, his appointments will be kept promptly, he will be as accessible as possible. In short, the president must have much of the same capacity an actor has of knowing how he appears to others, and will guide himself accordingly.

The energies which faculties and administrators waste in futile

[8] There does seem to be some evidence that faculty rivalries are keenest in those fields in which scholarship and opinions are least subject to objective tests of validity, in which truth, as Alexander Hamilton said, seems to be that which is loudly asserted and confidently maintained! President Hadley, after twenty-two years as president of Yale, generalized that (with exceptions) the members of the English and language faculties were frequently at odds, that differences were less frequent but more serious in history, economics, or law, that disputes were rare in the school of divinity, mathematics, or physics, but in the latter cases one always lost one contender or the other for each knew he was dealing with absolute truth! H. L. Donovan, "Changing Conceptions of the College Presidency," *Association of American Colleges Bulletin*, March 1957.

tugs-of-war can better be combined into efficient work by a clear, convincing philosophy of education than by any other device. Such a philosophy provides agreement as to purposes and program, a cause to the service of which personal differences and petty interests can be subordinated, a sense of mutual dependence and a respect for the essential services each performs.

When a president, within the limits of his intelligence and good will, has done everything he can to reduce institutional strains, he must further develop one of his essential qualifications for office—some philosophical resignation. What he cannot help he must accept. As President Ruthven, who for twenty-nine years presided imperturbably over the University of Michigan, said to a younger presidential associate, "Don't let it bother you. You didn't expect to be loved, did you?"

X

The Uses of a Philosophy of Education

THE MOST important qualification a college president can bring to his job is a philosophy of education. By a philosophy of education I mean nothing more than that he shall have thought about why the institution he presides over exists at all, for whom it is trying to provide education, and what kind of education it is trying to provide. The president will find such a philosophy has two indispensable uses: the first, to give the enterprise a sense of direction, the second, to serve him *every day* as a guide for administrative decisions. A college president without a philosophy of education is a pilot without navigation charts.[1]

Indeed, the initial impulses to found colleges always spring from some philosophy of education. New colleges arise because

[1] In discussing philosophies of education there is a danger of becoming pretentious. While there can be no objection to the possession of great philosophical skill in metaphysics, it is not necessary in order to acquire useful perspective as to the purposes an educational institution serves and the means it can appropriately use to serve them. See the comments of Sidney Hook, "The Scope of Philosophy of Education," *The Harvard Educational Review*, 1956, XXVI, pp. 145–148.

someone believes that there are those who are not now getting an education, or enough education, or the kind of education they should have. Consequently, there emerge such diverse institutions as the land-grant universities, Massachusetts Institute of Technology, Catholic University of America, Bennington College, and countless others. They embody in every case agreed upon educational convictions of sufficient concern to their holders to induce them to do something about them, namely to found a school. In fact, colleges always flourish best and always are most effective when their educational convictions are vigorous and in evidence.

While a philosophy of education is primarily a product of individual reflection, there are certain components which a college president in America will be compelled to incorporate in his personal philosophy if he wishes to be either successful or comfortable. Among these components are: a belief in education as salvation; an acceptance of education as an instrument of national policy; some views on educational utilitarianism; and some conclusions on the issue of classes versus masses. With his feet firmly planted on these basic concepts, the president is much less likely to be tossed about when the variable winds of educational doctrine blow.

These concepts deserve some extended examination.

Whatever may be the reasons, Americans have come to look upon education as a kind of instrument of salvation, both personal and national. It is the key to personal success, and the prescription for any national shortcoming from military weakness to juvenile delinquency is more education. The following declaration states our faith:

Without attempting here the impossibility of conclusive proof, I suggest that the American liberal arts college (including the church colleges) can find a significant, even unique, mission in the duality of its historic purpose: to see men made whole in *both* competence and conscience. Is there any other institution at the highest level of organized educational activity that is committed explicitly by its history and by its purpose to these twin goals?[2]

This view of educational salvation contributes substantially to the fundamentally optimistic character of American society, for it definitely places the power of our own salvation in our own hands. It makes education so inseparable a part of the progress in which we believe that the two are all but identical. Progress and education—education and progress; there must be no doubt about either. With his views based on an unshakable faith in the perfectibility of human nature, the educator firmly believes that time and devotion will enable intelligence—educated intelligence, that is—to solve all our problems. His optimism may even have an occasional note of desperation in it—as reflected in the previously quoted jeremiad of President Hutchins: "Education may not save us, but it is the only hope we have." Yet as a kind of social salvation education is an almost universal belief in America and no college president can hope to be effective unless he shares the belief and preaches it. Any doubts he may have he must keep to himself; indeed, he must do his best to exorcise them altogether.

This cheery optimism may be responsible for the label of "Rotarian" so often pinned to the college president,[3] but in the United States it must be accepted as the most important (as it is the most evident) single element of his educational philosophy. It is his declaration of faith; he would be absolutely lost without it. It gives him his sense of mission. It is what sustains his incessant efforts to raise money, to cultivate alumni and the public, to inspire students and the faculty. The president is fortunate whose

[2] John Sloan Dickey, "Conscience and the Undergraduate," *The Atlantic Monthly*, April 1955, p. 31.

[3] See Veblen's acid comments on these presidential attitudes, *The Higher Learning in America* (New York: Huebsch Co., 1918), pp. 88–90. He always referred to college presidents sarcastically as "captains of erudition," thus making them, by a phrase, analogous to "captains of industry," for whom he had less than respect.

convictions can happily be reinforced by an optimistic temperament and by his personal chemistry. The one indulgence he cannot permit himself or others is doubt as to the value and ultimate triumph of education. If he does, he will find himself completely disqualified for his job and thoroughly unhappy. In short, the college president must share the dominant sentiments of his generation, and education as salvation is one of this generation's most cherished articles of faith.

The second element which the president must incorporate into his philosophy of education relates to the purposes of higher education. Historically it is possible to identify in America three dominant or controlling purposes for education. The first was religious—for the glory of God. The second was what may be called the development of the individual—the Emersonian Man of Character. These two purposes have not disappeared from American education, but they have been joined and, to some extent, superseded by a third compelling purpose—the acceptance of education as an instrument of national policy.

While the view that higher education should be conducted so as to contribute to the strength of the nation is comparatively new, it has long been implicit. Under the impact of wars and technological change, this view has emerged swiftly. The dawning appreciation that education is an instrument of power on which survival itself depends has imposed upon education and upon educators a new obligation, superior to any other, namely, to keep the nation strong.

Stated so nakedly, the implications of the doctrine are a bit shocking but reflection softens the shock. There would be little education without national survival and there will be no national survival without education. It is easy to conclude that education must be enlisted in the service of the nation. The fact also that the contribution of the colleges and universities to the goal of national strength—military strength, to be specific—is so much greater and more direct than it used to be makes this compulsion irresistible. As military strength evolves more and more from scientific developments and becomes increasingly dependent upon the management and skill of educated persons, the colleges and universities naturally become more and more indispensable and more deeply involved.

As was mentioned earlier, there are more than five hundred colleges with officer training corps which during peacetime train more officers than do the army, navy, and air force, including the various military academies. The University of California operates Los Alamos and the University of Chicago operates the Argonne Laboratories for the federal government. Most of the physics departments of our major universities would shrink to shadows of themselves if not sustained by federal subsidies. Many other departments depend heavily upon the more than three hundred and fifty million dollars which the federal government annually spends among colleges and universities for research.

There is a growing recognition of the fact that the atomic age was not produced and cannot be sustained by uneducated people. This is why the national government through the National Science Foundation, the National Institutes of Health, and numerous other agencies, provides each year hundreds of fellowships for graduate students, refresher courses for teachers, and other forms of support for higher education. The debate over federal aid is beginning to sound as quaint to our ears as do the arguments of a generation ago about compulsory education.

The reorientation of our colleges and universities to the necessities of national interest, narrowly and urgently defined, is also reflected in their curricula. In such a social and political climate it becomes easy to encourage the development of studies and activities which relate directly to the national strength and to discourage or, at least, to neglect those whose direct contributions are not so clear; to support science, for example, but not philosophy. The "power" subjects flourish in such a climate, the contemplative subjects wither. The question of relevance takes on new significance. The classics and ancient history have virtually disappeared from the curriculum while English, history, and economics have adapted their offerings by large infusions of journalism, current social comment, and applied techniques. Mathematics, once scarcely more than a form of mental exercise for people with curious minds, now supplies a thrill of power to those who are trained in it.

Here then is a relatively new and compelling doctrine in the American philosophy of education. Developing as swiftly as it has, it has unquestionably bewildered many educators and placed a strain upon their habits and ideals. "Classified" work, for example, now finds acceptance on the campus, and students and professors in institutions which have always been devoted to freedom in the search for and use of knowledge now find it necessary to restrict their inquiries and conceal their results.

All of this, of course, produces problems for the college president. The moral issue is: how well does the service of the nation coincide with the service to mankind? How well does *Veritas*—the motto of every college, not of Harvard alone—fare under the limitations imposed by national necessity? The college president's educational philosophy will have to resolve such problems not only for himself but also for his institution. The claims of the national interest, he will find, must be met whether the college be public or private; the president must not only accept such claims as legitimate, he must do everything possible to help the institution meet them.

A third major component in a philosophy of education which a college president in America must be prepared to accept is the tenet that education of every kind must be useful. It is one of our most nearly universal measures of the value of education. If he is not compelled to subscribe to this tenet with quite the same orthodoxy with which he subscribes to the doctrine of national necessity, he will derive strength from fully sharing its vitality. I am here, of course, following Bacon's classification of knowledge as useful, enjoyable, or decorative. Knowledge for enjoyment and for decoration has been historically associated with a leisure class. But in America there is no leisure class. Everyone works—in some respects the economically well-to-do work hardest of all. In America, work is respectable; *not* to work calls for explanation and even apology. This is why education which is not useful, in the sense in which it is something which can be marketed or made of service to someone other than the person who possesses it, has little appeal.

This social requirement of utility is one of the most difficult handicaps which face the traditional liberal arts in trying to retain a central position in current education. It is extremely difficult to demonstrate the utility of history, literature, foreign languages, and even mathematics to a student interested in meeting the concerns of a society in a type of education which is immediately marketable. No matter how much lip service may be paid, either inside or outside the college walls, to the ideals of learning and culture, the student senses quickly enough the greater interest in what he can *do*, rather than in what he *knows*. The colleges and universities, themselves subject to the same compelling social forces which govern the students' interests, make accommodations in their curricula, the development of their facilities, and in the methods and materials of instruction. If learning cannot convincingly demonstrate its contribution to competence, it will be in danger of being relegated to the small and irrelevant concerns of leisure-time activities.

A fourth philosophical issue on which the college president must possess some articulate views is an answer to the question, "Who shall be educated?" It is, in innocent form, the question of education and democracy, the few or the many, the masses or the classes. It is one of the oldest, most persistent, and most pervasive of all educational debates. As an issue it appears to contain all others within it.

From the days of the Greeks it has been an accepted tradition that education should devote itself to the discovery and development of excellence. In every society some minds are superior to others and it has always been thought a responsibility of education to discover these superior minds and to develop their special qualities—as the Greeks called them, "virtues."

Much of the paraphernalia of modern educational management reflects this conception. Our devices for differentiating between students—aptitude and intelligence tests, competitive examinations, grades, and scholarships—are devices to sift out of our society the minds of distinction. Registrars and admissions officers are agents of this philosophy of education.

This clear, single-minded interest in excellence dominated American higher education for a long time. Even Jefferson looked upon the public school system as a device for "raking over the rubbish" in order that the "best geniuses" might be discovered and given further instruction. Yet by the beginning of the nineteenth century such clarity of purpose began to be blurred by new democratic ideas about human nature and the rights of man. Equality, rather than inequality, began to be emphasized, the characteristics which men had in common rather than the things which made each distinctive. The philosophy of the Declaration of Independence invaded education as well as politics—all men were created equal with rights to life, liberty, and the pursuit of happiness.

It was a fairly logical step, even if long in the taking, for education to begin to occupy itself, if not less with the cultivation of excellence, at least more with the happiness of all. In the verse of William Watson:

THE USES OF A PHILOSOPHY OF EDUCATION

> Momentous to himself, as I to me,
> Hath each man been, that woman ever bore.
> Once, in a lightning flash of sympathy
> I felt this truth, an instant and no more.

This was the new insight, a "lightning flash of sympathy," which made the happiness of each as important as the happiness of any. Educationally it would eventually mean "education for all," the view that each has an equal right to whatever education is appropriate to his talents. This is the democratic philosophy of education.[4]

These two great basic and conflicting points of view struggle constantly for ascendancy in American higher education. The debate rages within every college and university, every department, and, indeed, in the breast of almost every educator. English departments, for example, are constantly torn by their concern for future "scholars" on the one hand and their desire to "serve" a larger number on the other. Are they teaching "literature" or "communication"? Should departments of music teach music appreciation or concentrate on the development of performing artists? Should departments of physical education devote themselves to athletes or to the cause of recreation? Should history be taught as a field of scholarship or to make good citizens?

As long as American colleges and universities are engaged in providing education either for the few or the many or both, their presidents will be compelled to formulate their views on the subject. The debate cannot be isolated. It will force its way into discussion of admission policies, curricula, appeals for financial

---

[4] A report of the Education Policies Commission of the National Education Association entitled "Education for All American Youth," while recognizing individual differences, says eloquently: "Each of them is a human being, more precious than material goods, or systems of philosophy. Not one of them is to be carelessly wasted. All of them are to be given equal opportunity to live and learn" (1944 ed.), p. 18.

support. Perhaps no other question will appear before a president in so many different disguises.

Here, then, are four major components, some understanding of which every college president must incorporate into his philosophy of education—a faith in education as salvation; the doctrine of national necessity; the acceptance of utility; and views on education and democracy. There are, of course, other elements even more fundamental philosophically, such as one's belief in the rationality of mankind. But if a president has his views of these tough and recurrent questions well in hand he will be "administratively operational" and reasonably comfortable intellectually.

Nor should any college president think his views on these subjects too vague and general for practical use. He will need them in answering his mail, in his faculty conferences, in his public addresses. An irate alumnus writes that refusal of admission to his son "denies a right open to every American." A department proposes "to strengthen its offering" because it believes its students need more "practical" work. The college sends a representative to Washington to arrange for a construction loan for a new dormitory. A research contract requires that a part of a university building be kept under constant armed guard. A member of the board of trustees has just announced that in his opinion "this college is big enough" and there are "too many people going to college anyhow." In every instance a philosophy of education is involved. If, in each instance, the president understands the philosophical context, he will find himself able to deal with the situation more wisely. He will, at least, have provided himself some philosophical protection against fretting.

The most practical use a college president can make of a philosophy of education is to unite a campus and reduce its sense of conflict—conflict not only within a faculty but also between faculty and administration. As the specialization of knowledge increases, the preoccupation of faculty members with their special fields grows more intense. The more intent each is upon his own, the less is his interest in others and in the total process. The very dedication of the teacher and scholar can thus paradoxically become a source of internal tension, rivalry, and misunderstanding.

Consequently, it becomes more and more a responsibility of the president to supply the campus with its unifying force. People close ranks in a common cause; the president of the college must state the common cause so clearly and convincingly that biologists, historians, linguists, and athletic coaches can be enlisted. The responsibility of the university president is here even greater and more difficult than that of the college president. The common cause of the university must be made to include doctors, lawyers, engineers, dentists, social workers, business administrators, and a host of special interests. To what possible common denominators of tradition, knowledge, public service, or ethical purpose can a university president appeal which will pull such diverse interests together?

Whatever they are, the president will have to find them. He will have to state them so persuasively that each teacher, scholar, and administrator can see in their fulfillment his own educational mission. A college is an organic, not merely a composite, enterprise which should operate on a basis of consensus rather than upon legal regulations which grow out of political relationships. Such consensus exists only where there is a clear sense of duty and of obligation, agreement about the ends to be served, and the means appropriate to serve them. This is a higher conception of an institution than one operating under a system of checks and balances in which the president serves as an arbiter between opposing and competing parties at interest. It is the president's tremendously difficult task to describe the whole so that it is intelligible to each of its parts. If he succeeds, his inner sense of reward will be as great as the magnitude of the service he has performed.

A Bibliographical Note

There are comparatively few books and articles which deal directly with either the nature of the office of the college president or of the persons who hold it. College presidents while in office are so busy being college presidents that they have little time or inclination to write about their work. Their contributions (many times excellent) to the understanding of their position must be derived for the most part from their essays and addresses on education and related matters. A few eminent presidents have written autobiographies, but the focus of these books is quite naturally the career of a man, not the description of an office. Representative citations of such literature follow.

A more pertinent source of presidential discussions of the office is to be found in annual institutional reports which many presidents prepare for their boards of trustees, alumni, legislatures, or the general public. Some of these are rich in educational philosophy and administrative comment. President Robert M. Hutchins, while at Chicago, wrote some particularly thoughtful and provocative reports; the same has been true of Presidents Conant of Harvard, Dodds of Princeton, and Sproul of California, to mention only a few examples from a notable body of educational commentary.

Most of the material about the college presidency must be gathered from writings about higher education and from discussions of general management and administration. From innumerable discussions about the nature and work of colleges and universities, there can be distilled notions as to the role of their presidents. Writers in the field of general and educational administration have also found in the college presidency aspects of management which interest them—the study of organization, personnel and financial administration, public relations, and the like. There is now a journal, *College and University Business*, which is devoted to the growing business concerns of higher education.

Two older books deserve special mention: Abraham Flexner, *Universities: American, English and German*, and Thorsten Veblen, *The Higher Learning in America*. Veblen's book is the more penetrating and trenchant so far as the administration of American higher education is concerned. Thoughtful as they are, however, both books show strong preference for European models and reject much that is indigenous not only to American higher education but to the American way of life. The low estimate made by these authors of higher education in America has unfortunately been accepted too widely and too long by many European intellectuals.

The following citations are intended only to assist the reader to find his way to wider sources.

American Council on Education, *Faculty-Administration Relationships*, a report by the Commission on Instruction and Evaluation, 1958.

James B. Angell, *The Reminiscences of James Burrill Angell*, Longmans, Green and Co., New York, 1912.

Laird Bell, "From the Trustees' Corner," *Association of American Colleges Bulletin*, October 1956.

Nicholas Murray Butler, *Across the Busy Years: Recollections and Reflections*, 2 vols., Charles Scribner's Sons, New York, 1940.

R. Freeman Butts, *The College Charts Its Course*, McGraw-Hill Co., New York, 1939.

Samuel P. Capen, *The Management of Universities*, Foster and Stewart Publishing Co., Buffalo, 1953.

College and University Business Administration, 2 vols., American Council on Education, Washington, 1952–55.

Edmund E. Day, "The Role of Administration in Higher Education," *Journal of Higher Education*, October 1946.

Marshall E. Dimock, *A Philosophy of Administration*, Harper & Bros., New York, 1958.

P. F. Douglass, "Conant's Concept of University Administration," *Journal of Higher Education*, February 1954.

Charles W. Eliot, *University Administration*, Houghton Mifflin Co., New York, 1908.

———, *A Late Harvest*, Atlantic Monthly Press, Boston, 1924.

Abraham Flexner, *Universities, American, English, German*, Oxford University Press, New York, 1930.

Daniel Coit Gilman, *The Launching of the University*, Dodd, Mead and Co., New York, 1906.

R. J. Havighurst, "Governing the University," *School and Society*, March 1954.

Richard Hofstadter and Walter P. Metzger, *The Development of Academic Freedom in the United States*, Columbia University Press, New York, 1955.

Ernest Martin Hopkins, *This Our Purpose*, Dartmouth Publications, 1950.

Robert M. Hutchins, "The Administrator," *Journal of Higher Education*, November 1946.

———, *No Friendly Voice*, Louisiana State University Press, 1936.

David Starr Jordan, *The Voice of the Scholar*, P. Elder and Co., San Francisco, 1903.

Dexter M. Keezer, *The Light That Flickers*, Harper & Bros., New York, 1947.

Norman Kiell, "Periodical Literature on the College President, 1932–1957," *School and Society*, April 12, 1958.

A BIBLIOGRAPHY NOTE

A. Lawrence Lowell, *What A University President Has Learned*, The Macmillan Co., New York, 1938.

"The Rights and Responsibilities of Universities and Their Faculties," A Statement by the *Association of American Universities*, 1953.

Beardsley Ruml and Sidney G. Tickton, *Teaching Salaries Then and Now*, Fund for the Advancement of Education, New York, 1955.

Clarence A. Schoenfeld, *The University and Its Publics*, Harper & Bros., New York, 1954.

Upton Sinclair, *The Goose Step, A Study of American Education*, A. and C. Boni, New York, 1923.

Harold Taylor, *On Education and Freedom*, Abelard–Schuman, New York, 1926.

Ordway Tead, *Trustees, Teachers, Students, Their Role in the University*, University of Utah Press, 1951.

———, *The Art of Administration*, McGraw-Hill Co., New York, 1951.

Charles W. Thwing, *The College President*, The Macmillan Co., New York, 1926.

Thorsten Veblen, *The Higher Learning in America*, Huebsch Co., New York, 1918.

Harry L. Wells, *Higher Education Is Serious Business*, Harper & Bros., New York, 1953.

Logan Wilson, *The Academic Man*, Oxford University Press, 1942.

Henry M. Wriston, *The Nature of a Liberal College*, Lawrence College Press, 1937.

———, *Wriston Speaking*, Brown University Press, Providence, 1957.

Index

Academic freedom, 75, 112–113
Adams, Henry, *quoted*, 23, 121, 147
Administration, definition of, 34
  pathology of, 157–158
Administrator, president as, 34–53
Alumni, 95–100
  and prospective students, 98
  as trustees, 73, 98
Amherst College, 101
Angell, James B., 17 *n.*
Argonne Laboratories, 165
Aristotle, *quoted*, 24
Association of American Colleges, 125 *n.*
Association of American Universities, 24, 125 *n.*
Athletics:
  as entertainment, 7, 101
  football, 7, 92, 101
  a moral problem, 103
  and public relations, 100–103
  under student control, 102–103

Bacon, Francis, 19 f., 167
Bagehot, Walter, *quoted*, 124
Bell, Laird, *quoted*, 86–87
Bemus, Edward W., *quoted*, 153–154
Bennington College, 162
"Big-university" pattern, 118
Bridges, Harry, 37
Brougham, Lord, *quoted*, 33
Budget, 61–63
  see also Finances
Bureaucracy, 151–152
Business manager, 64

Butler, Nicholas Murray, 17, 107
  quoted, 116–117

Cabinet system, 43
California, University of, 11, 17, 37, 74 f., 92, 139
  athletics at, 102
  budget for, 4, 60
  federal subsidies for, 7, 165
  loyalty oath at, 80
  See also U.C.L.A.
Carnegie Corporation, 13 *n.*, 14 *n.*, 20
Catholic University of America, 162
Chicago, University of, 11 *n.*, 16, 76
  federal subsidies for, 165
  football at, 92, 101
  reorganization of, 80, 126, 140
  staff appointments at, 85 *n.*
"Child-centered" society, 132, 137
Church-related colleges, 4, 73
Clark, Jonas Gilman, 75
Clark University, 75
Coffman, Louis D., *quoted*, 34
College president, the
  as administrator, 34–53
  and alumni, 95–100
  authority vested in, 1–2
  and board of trustees, 76 ff.
  as a business man, 35–36
  and campus interests, 141
  discoveries of, 21 ff.
  "duty speeches" by, 94
  and educational leadership, 125–126, 140, 142
  and faculty, 106–128

conflict with, 151–154
selection of, 117–120
family of, 28 f.
freedom of speech for, 22–23
and friendships, 23–24
fringe benefits for, 28
functions of, 10
and information, 43–46, 49, 62
ministers as, 2
moral qualities of decisions of, 53
nonacademic, 17 *n.*
personal problems of, 21–33
personality of, shaped by occupation, 30, 158
precariousness of tenure, 17, 18–19
and public relations, 89–105
qualities and qualifications of, 2–3, 13–17
and retirements and resignations, 18 *n.*
selection of, 11–12
and the students, 129–145
contacts with, 134–136
social life of, institutional, 30–31
a unifying force, 171
"visibility" of, 14 *n.*, 32
Colleges and universities, *see* Church-related colleges, Higher education, Land grant colleges, Private colleges, State colleges
See also Amherst, Bennington, California, Catholic University of America, Chicago, Clark, Colorado, Columbia, Cornell, Dartmouth, Fordham, Harvard, Idaho, Illinois, Johns Hopkins, Kenyon, Louisiana State, Massachusetts Institute of Technology, Michigan, Mills, Minnesota, New York, North Carolina, Northwestern, Notre Dame, Oberlin, Ohio State, Oklahoma, Park, Pennsylvania, Pittsburgh, Princeton, Reed, Stanford, Swarthmore, Texas, Tulane, U.C.L.A., Wabash, Washington, Western Reserve, William and Mary, Williams, Wisconsin, Yale
Colorado, University of, 92
Columbia University, 7, 16 f., 92
Commercialism, 8–9
Communism, 80, 114
Conant, James Bryant, 16, 19 *n.*, 24, 126, 172
Coolidge, Charles A., *quoted*, 88
Cornell University, 73, 75
Curriculum, 67, 165

Dartmouth College, 2, 17, 19 *n.*, 97
Deans, 42
Delegation of responsibility, 38, 40
Democracy, 120, 167–170
Deutsch, Monroe, *quoted*, 17 *n.*
Dickey, John Sloane, 19 *n.*
 quoted, 130–131, 163
Dodds, Harold W., 172
Due process, 49–51
Dykstra, Clarence Addison, *quoted*, 20

Education, adult, 6–7
compulsory, ix
See also Higher education, Philosophy of education
Education Policies Commission, 169 *n.*
Eisenhower, Dwight D., 16
Eliot, Charles W., 2, 17 *n.*, 107
 quoted, 52 f., 156
Erskine, John, *quoted*, 20

Faculty, 106–128
and board of trustees, 79–85
committees, 79
and finances, 66–67
job security for, 115
participation in the administration, 120–124
personality traits of, 115–116
and president, 107–110, 126, 151–154
rivalry among, 111

INDEX

salaries, 109–110
selection of, 117–120
Fait accompli, art of the, 46–47
Federal subsidies, 7, 165–166
Finances, 54–70
  budget, 61–63
  cost accounting, 69 f.
  discretionary funds, 60
  faculty responsibility, 66–67
  faculty salaries, 109–110
  fringe benefits, 65
  fund-raising, 59–60, 93
  public vs. private institutions, 56–58
  tuition, 55
Flexner, Abraham, 173
Fordham University, 102
Frank, Glenn, 126
Fringe benefits, 28, 65
Fulbright, Sen. William, 32

G.I. Bill of Rights, 5
Gilman, Daniel Coit, 17 *n.*, 119 *n.*
  quoted, 117
Goheen, Robert F., 17
Goosestep, The (Sinclair), 75
Griswold, A. Whitney, 16

Hadley, Arthur Twining, *quoted*, 159 *n.*
Hamilton, Alexander, *quoted*, 159 *n.*
Harper, William Rainey, 17 *n.*, 107, 119 *n.*
  quoted, 154
Harvard University, 2, 16, 19 *n.*, 73, 126
  finances, 4, 35, 54, 66, 93
  summer institute for college presidents, 13 *n.*
Higher education:
  as big business, 4
  changes in, 6–10
  commercialism in, 8–9
  federal government in, 7, 165–166
  purposes of, 142, 144, 164
  after World War II, 5, 24

Higher Education is Serious Business, 69 *n.*
Higher Learning in America, The (Veblen), 68 *n.*, 173
Hiss, Alger, 37
Hopkins, Ernest Martin, 17, 19 *n.*, 40, 76
Hutchins, Robert Maynard, 16, 24, 52, 56, 80, 107, 126, 140, 172
  quoted, 3, 55, 108–109, 163
Huxley, Thomas H., *quoted*, 143

Idaho, College of, 11 *n.*
Illinois, University of, 7, 17, 35, 80
Information, giving of, 49, 62
  president's need for, 43–46

James, William, 111, 148
Jefferson, Thomas, *quoted*, 168
Jessup, Walter, 20
Johns Hopkins University, 17, 58 *n.*, 76, 102
Jordan, David Starr, 17 *n.*, 107, 119 *n.*

Keppel, Francis P., *quoted*, 116
Kenyon College, 92
Killian, James R., 17

Land-grant colleges, 31, 75, 162
Little, Clarence Cook, 16
Los Alamos, 165
"Loyalty laughter," 21
Loyalty oath, 80
Louisiana State University, 74, 91
Lynd, Robert S., 76 *n.*

MacArthur, Douglas, 38
Mann, Horace, 4
Massachusetts Institute of Technology, 7, 17, 91, 162
Merry, Robert W., 13 *n.*
Michigan, University of, 7, 16, 101
Mills College, 54
Minnesota, University of, 91
Morrill, James L., 102

INDEX

National Association of State Universities, 18, 125 *n.*
National Education Association, 169 *n.*
National Institutes of Health, 165
National Science Foundation, 165
New York University, 92, 101 f.
North Carolina, University of, 139
Northwestern University, 102
Notre Dame, University of, 59 *n.*, 92, 101

Oberlin College, 92
O'Hara, John, 11 *n.*
Ohio State University, 96 *n.*
Oklahoma, University of, 91
Oppenheimer, J. Robert, *quoted*, 148

Paine, Thomas, 3
Park, George S., *quoted*, 82–83
Park College, 83 *n.*
Pennsylvania, University of, 16
Philosophy of education, 161–171
Pittsburgh, University of, 102
Princeton University, 2, 17, 37, 97, 140
Private colleges, 4, 74
Public relations, 89–105
 and alumni, 95–100
 and athletics, 100–103
 defensive (protective), 90–91
 and fund-raising, 93
 promotional
Pusey, Nathan M., 16, 19 *n.*, 66

Reed College, 101
Rivalry, 68, 111, 149–151
Rockefeller, John D., 75
R.O.T.C., 6, 165
Rousseau, *quoted*, 22
Ruml, Beardsley, *quoted*, 38, 112
Ruthven, Alexander M., 16
 quoted, 160

Shakespeare, 10 *n.*
Shorey, Paul, *quoted*, 120 *n.*

Sinclair, Upton, 75
Social life, institutional, 30–31
Speakers, visiting, 37
Specialists, 10
Speech, freedom of, 22–23
Sproul, Robert G., 17, 56, 80, 172
Stanford, Senator and Mrs., 75
Stanford University, 75, 97
Stassen, Harold E., 17
State colleges, 73 ff., 135
Stoddard, George D., 80
Students, 129–145
 administration of, 131
 college a social event for, 136–137
 contacts with president, 134–136
 immaturity of, 138
 participation in administration, 138–139
 rating of professors by, 138
Superintendent of property, 64
Swarthmore College, 11

Teaching, 147
Tead, Ordway, *quoted*, 79
Tensions, campus, 146–160
 sources of, 147, 156–157
Tenure, 42, 115
Texas, University of, 93
Tickton, Sidney G., *quoted*, 112
Tressider, Donald B., 18 *n.*
Trevelyan, George Macaulay, *quoted*, 24–25
Trustees, boards of, 71–88
 alumni representation on, 73, 98
 appointment of staff, 83–85
 composition of, 74
 faculty representation on, 79
 and finance, 81–82
 and "housekeeping" problems, 81
 and the president, 12, 76–78
 size of, 73
 term of office, 74
 unity, necessity for, 87
Tuition, 55
 see also Finances
Tulane University, 102

U.C.L.A., 91, 101
  see also California, University of
Universities, see Colleges and universities
Universities: American, English and German (Flexner), 173

Veblen, Thorsten, 152 *n.*, 173
  quoted, 68 *n.*, 163 *n.*

Wabash College, 92
Walpole, the elder, *quoted*, 15
Warren, R. L., 150 *n.*
Washington, George, 3
Washington, University of, 92, 102, 139

Watson, William, *quoted*, 168–169
Wells, Harry L., *quoted*, 69 *n.*
Western Reserve University, 101 f.
Wheeler, Benjamin Ide, 17 *n.*
Whyte, William H., Jr., *quoted*, 149, *n.*, 150 *n.*
William and Mary, College of, 60
Williams College, 101
Wilson, Woodrow, 2, 107
  quoted, 43, 140, 149 *n.*
Wisconsin, University of, 28, 79, 126
World War II, 5, 24
Wriston, Henry M., *quoted*, 114

Yale University, 2, 17
Young, Robert, 150 *n.*

Stoke, Harold Walter, 1903–
 The American college president. [1st ed.] New York, Harper [1959]
 180 p. 22 cm.

 1. College presidents.   I. Title.

LB2341.S8   378.11   58–13232 ‡
Library of Congress